TASTY

over
the
top

# TASTY™

## over the top

### HIGH DRAMA, LOW MAINTENANCE

**Clarkson Potter/Publishers**

New York

Published in the United States by Clarkson Potter/Publishers, an imprint of Random House, a division of Penguin Random House LLC, New York.

clarksonpotter.com

CLARKSON POTTER is a trademark and POTTER with colophon is a registered trademark of Penguin Random House LLC.

TASTY is trademark of Buzzfeed, Inc., and used under license. All rights reserved.

Some recipes originally appeared on Tasty.co.

Library of Congress Cataloging-in-Publication Data
Names: Buzzfeed Inc., editor.
Title: Tasty over the top: high drama, low maintenance.
Description: New York, NY: Clarkson Potter/Publishers [2021] | Includes index.
Identifiers: LCCN 2020052983 (print) | LCCN 2020052984 (ebook) | ISBN 9780593233474 (hardcover) | ISBN 9780593233481 (ebook)
Subjects: LCSH: Quick and easy cooking. | LCGFT: Cookbooks.
Classification: LCC TX833.5 .T38 2021 (print) | LCC TX833.5 (ebook) | DDC 641.5/12—dc23
LC record available at https://lccn.loc.gov/2020052983
LC ebook record available at https://lccn.loc.gov/2020052984

ISBN 978-0-593-23347-4

eBook ISBN 978-0-593-23348-1

Printed in China

Photographer: Lauren Volo
Designer: Ashley Tucker
Art directors: Jen Wang, Robert Diaz
Editor: Raquel Pelzel
Assistant editor: Lydia O'Brien
Editorial assistant: Bianca Cruz
Production editor: Mark McCauslin
Production manager: Heather Williamson
Compositor: Merri Ann Morrell, Nick Patton
Indexer: Elizabeth T. Parson

10 9 8 7 6 5 4 3 2 1

First Edition

# CONTENTS

# INTRODUCTION

**First things first:** let's define *Over the Top*. Does "over the top" mean these are impossible recipes that require flawless technique and lots of equipment? Um, no, that book does not sound like fun at all. Does "over the top" mean you'll be putting things on top of things? Yeah, that definitely happens here. There are also things *in* things, plus lots of drizzling and stuffing. But no, that's not really the point either. Does "over the top" mean you'll be exploring flavors, presentations, and combinations you've never considered? Yes! That you'll tackle things that are wild beyond belief but still totally doable? Oh yes! That these recipes will encourage you to question everything you've always known to be true *and* mark the moment that begins now, your new life, full of over-the-top food? Yaaaassss!!! That's absolutely what this book is all about.

"Over the top" can even be a small thing—often a simple thing—that makes the everyday extraordinary, such as Tomato Soup in a Grilled Cheese Bread Bowl (whaaaat? see page 60), Peanut Butter & Jelly Donuts (flip to page 34 to flip out), a Milkshake Overload that you have to see to believe (check the photo on page 134), or a Grilled BLT Salad (head to page 72) that has everything you love from the sandwich but in a salad. In this book, you'll find 75 recipes that will blow your mind with their creativity, sneaky hacks, and *Over the Top* deliciousness.

While the recipes score big on flavor and creativity, they stay simple on ingredients and execution. For example, you may be making a Cheez-It Quiche, but you're doing it with just six main ingredients (page 36, pronto!). Or a BBQ Sheet Pan Supper that's just a matter of wrapping things in foil and baking them all together on a sheet pan with collards, mac, ribs, and all (giddyup to page 81). Or—get this—a Salad Party Platter that's as easy as unwrapping a few items, popping some lids, and laying salad ingredients on a table, but it's also literally the most elegant thing you've ever seen (the glow-up starts on page 92). You'll see a lot of packets, jars, cans, bags, and boxes of common grocery items throughout the book. It's definitely a working-smarter-not-harder vibe in these pages.

When it comes to plating these treats, now is the time to go big and go bold. Over the top is a total mood. It's confetti, sparklers, little cocktail umbrellas, *RuPaul's Drag Race*, gel pens, WWE, mood rings, Jock Jams, Lisa Frank, T-shirt cannons, gold lamé, muscle cars, K-pop stans, Britney's Instagram, hot dog eating contests, roller coasters, and tacky pool floats. Does that make sense? Don't worry about it! Grab your wildest dish and dress it up, pile it on, glitter it, sauce it, garnish it. (That's the big.) Or reject the flair and let the food speak for itself. (That's the bold.) Sometimes a simple plating can be the most stunning presentation, and the surprise is all in the first bite. Or sometimes a truly insane plating can be like, "Ayo, bro get a pic of me for the 'gram real quick." There's no wrong way, only creative perspectives.

What's most important is having fun. These recipes are meant to spark your imagination, make you laugh, make you think, and make you question what food can be. Go in with an open mind and see where it takes you. Nothing is that serious, most of all food, so start cooking with a wink and a little flair. That's the real meaning of "over the top"!

# the TURBOCHARGED pantry

On the following pages, you'll find all the basics, plus the party. Most of these ingredients can be purchased fairly inexpensively and have long shelf lives, so that "over the top" doesn't become "overbudget."

## Fats

**Extra-virgin olive oil.** There are delicious and inexpensive brands of extra-virgin olive oil in the grocery store, perfect for everyday cooking. For an over-the-top edge, invest in a bottle of extra-delicious extra-virgin to use for dipping and drizzling only.

**Vegetable oil.** With a light flavor and high smoke point, vegetable oil is perfect to use whenever you are deep-frying, stir-frying, and high-heat cooking.

**Peanut oil.** With a pleasant peanutty flavor and very high smoke point, peanut oil is perfect for the heaviest heavy-duty frying.

**Unsalted butter.** Stick with unsalted so you can control the sodium levels in your food. Investing in good butter is one way to take a dish over the top. Another way is to make your own butter. A third way is to buy a cow. jkjkjk.

## Acids

**Red wine vinegar.** Super flavorful, red wine vinegar adds a lot of punch to any dish. Use it to stand up to (or cut through) big, rich flavors.

**White wine vinegar.** Good for dressing delicate salads and lighter meats.

**Apple cider vinegar.** An unmistakable sweet-tart flavor that is great for accenting sweet and savory dishes alike.

## Condiments

**Tamari.** Tamari is a Japanese variation of soy sauce. It offers a more savory flavor than the salty punch of Chinese soy sauce, and is often gluten-free (check the label to be sure).

**Dijon mustard.** Forget all other mustards—this is the one. Dressings, sauces, and sandwiches will get a ton of flavor, without an overpowering mustard aftertaste.

**Yellow mustard and grainy Dijon mustard.** Okay, forget what we just said about forgetting other mustards. Yellow mustard is the best for when you need an unmistakable classic ballpark mustard flavor. If it's texture you're after, you can't beat the crunch of grainy Dijon. These two are great to have on hand.

**Mayonnaise.** Mayo is a secret weapon for adding a ton of flavor and holding everything together.

**Ketchup.** Not just for burgers, ketchup is great for adding savory acidity to sauces and glazes.

**Hot sauce.** Hot sauce can range from taco-truck-style habanero to the ubiquitous squeeze bottle of sriracha. Pick one that you love for everyday use and grab a couple other styles to meet the needs of specific dishes. (But let's be honest, if you're a Hot

Sauce Person, your collection is probably already over the top.)

**Honey.** Honey can be expensive, but it's worth it to invest in a good bottle, preferably from somewhere local. If you're going to branch out from clover, wildflower, or orange blossom, go really over the top with something wild like spicy honey!

**Peanut butter.** Good old PB can bridge sweet and savory dishes, so it's always good to have on hand. And by "good" we mean everything from natural brands to your favorite childhood brand, whatever you like best.

**Jams and fruit preserves.** Fruit jams are for so much more than just toast and sandwiches! Keep a few flavors around for dressing up everything from breakfast to dessert (and making cocktails, too).

## Dry Goods

**Pasta.** Keep a few boxes of various pastas in fun shapes around.

**Rice.** Similar to pasta, rice comes in a lot of fun varieties, from jet-black Forbidden Rice to multicolored mixes. Keep a couple varieties, like long-grain white, a short-grain type, and some brown rice, on hand at all times.

**Bread crumbs.** Perfect for binding, coating, and topping, dried bread crumbs are a triple threat worth keeping around. Buy plain; you can take it over the top with herbs and spices as needed. (Extra over-the-top move: pulverizing a stale nub of bread in the food processor, then stashing those homemade crumbs in the freezer.)

**Flour.** All-purpose is the standard, and that's all we'll use here.

**Baking soda and baking powder.** Both are leavening agents, but they react differently. Baking soda reacts to acid, so the rise begins immediately. Baking powder reacts to acid and heat, so the reaction starts immediately, but the rise happens in the oven. Note that they cannot be used interchangeably, even though they're often used together. And hey, do your baking projects a solid and swap out your baking powder supply every 6 to 12 months.

**Granulated sugar.** The standard for sweetener. This is the white sugar you're used to seeing.

**Light brown sugar.** Brown sugar is granulated sugar mixed with molasses. Light brown sugar has a more subtle flavor than dark, giving it a higher adaptability and broader application.

**Powdered sugar.** The perfect finishing touch when breakfast or dessert needs some over-the-top flair, and essential for glazes and frostings. It's sometimes labeled "icing sugar" or "confectioners' sugar."

## Seasonings

**Salt.** Salting well is step one to making over-the-top flavors sing. Kosher salt has a nice texture for easy seasoning and isn't aggressively salty. (Plus, it's cheap in bulk!) Also invest in a good flaky sea salt, like Maldon or Jacobsen, for finishing touches on sweet and savory alike.

**Pepper.** Buy a sturdy pepper grinder and refill it with whole peppercorns as needed. Nothing beats freshly ground pepper—the oils in the peppercorns activate for an extra-pepper-y taste; plus, you can control the grind from fine to coarse.

**Dried herbs and spices.** Dried herbs are much more powerful than fresh, so reduce the quantity called for by a third if subbing in dried. Dried spices in general are best when heat and fat can activate their flavor (known as blooming), so make sure they interact with heat at some point while using them. If yours have been around since the last Tasty book hit shelves, it's probably time to replace them.

## Fresh

**Meats, produce, herbs, and dairy** should be purchased as close as possible to the day you'll need them. Buying meat in bulk can be cheaper in the long run, so portion and freeze what you don't immediately need.

Just remember to move it to the refrigerator at least twelve hours before you need it so it has time to defrost.

Similarly, **frozen fruit** can be useful in months when fresh is out of season.

Buying **vegetables and herbs** in small quantities may seem tedious, but it's cheaper than throwing them out after a few days. Some frozen vegetables, like peas and corn, are often tastier and easier than buying fresh.

**Cheese, milk, and eggs** should all be bought as needed to prevent spoilage. Shredded cheese can be frozen and thawed later, but everything else should be used before the expiration date.

# OVER THE TOP *pantry*

Beyond the basics, keep a shelf or a drawer full of the fun stuff to add a burst of party spirit to any dish.

**Sprinkles.** They all have a home here: everything from nonpareils (tiny multicolored balls) to classic rainbow to glistening sanding sugar to edible glitter.

**Candy.** A variety of things like mini candy bars, peanut butter cups, gummy candies, lollipops, sour candies, marshmallows, and chocolate chips will give desserts and drinks an over-the-top decorative and celebratory boost.

**Cookies.** The classics—like graham crackers, vanilla wafers, chocolate sandwich cookies, and toaster pastries—can be crushed and crumbled for a variety of applications, like a crunchy finish to a dessert, a delicious rim on a milkshake glass, or a sweet surprise at breakfast.

**Chips.** To add texture and flavor to savory dishes, keep everything from sour cream and onion to flamin' hot to nacho cheese. They'll all come in handy whether you're building the ultimate nachos, turbocharging corn on the cob, or making an over-the-top omelet.

**Butterfly pea flower tea.** Butterfly pea flower tea is a popular herbal tea in Southeast Asia that is just starting to show up in Western stores. Vibrant blue when brewed, it turns a beautiful pale lavender when lemon juice is added. Search for it in specialty tea shops or order it online. Make sure to buy the dried flowers, not the powder.

**Matcha green tea powder.** It feels like everything on Instagram is matcha-colored these days. Source this Japanese tea from specialty tea shops or order it online. We prefer packets of presweetened matcha powder.

**Pitaya powder.** Pitaya, also commonly known as dragon fruit, creates an electric pink powder. Many health food stores have started carrying this superfood powder (it's great in smoothies!), and it's also easy to find online

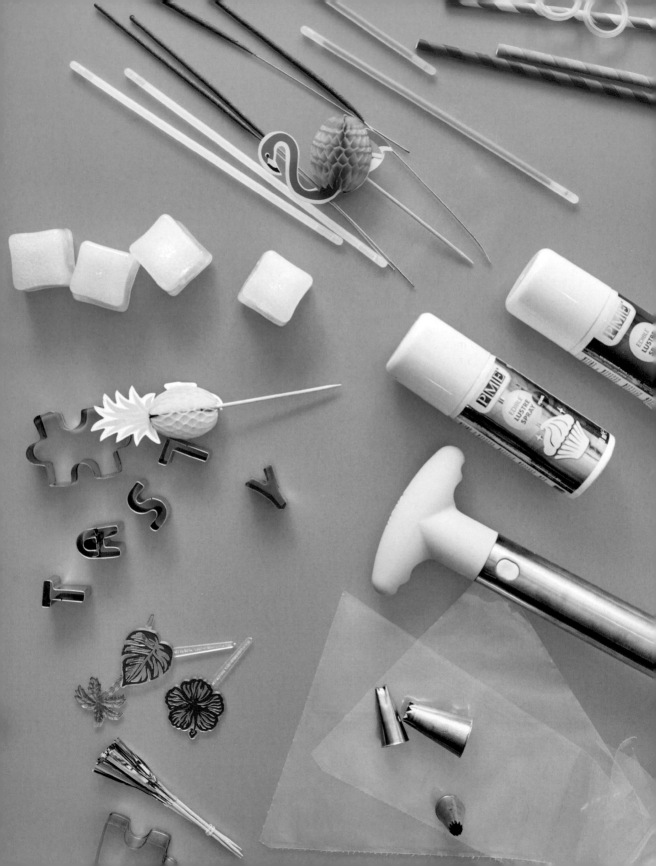

# *kitchen* TO THE MAX

## The Basics

Let's start with the basics. Shop around (or read reviews!) to find the intersection of cheap and well-made tools. Every kitchen should have . . .

**Measuring spoons.** Preferably ranging from ¼ teaspoon to 1 tablespoon (spoons with elongated scoops are convenient for dipping into spice jars).

**Measuring cups.** Dry measuring cups ranging from ¼ cup to 1 cup and a liquid measuring cup that holds 2 cups.

**Cutting board.** Go big, sturdy, and nonslip. Don't worry about having separate ones for meat, fish, and vegetables—just wash your cutting board well between uses. Plastic is easy to throw in the dishwasher, while wood easily doubles as a perfect serving platter for everything from cheese to grilled meats.

**Fine-mesh strainer.** Get a large one for draining pasta, rinsing beans, and sprinkling powdered sugar. Its uses are endless.

**Chef's knife.** This is practically the only knife you need. It doesn't have to be expensive, just make sure it's a comfortable size and weight for you—you'll be using it a lot. A dull knife puts you in danger of slippage and accidents, so also invest in a knife sharpener to keep it in prime shape (or find out where you can have it sharpened).

**Paring knife.** This is much smaller than a chef's knife and is ideal for precise tasks like trimming or making small slices.

**Wooden spoon.** Gentle enough to stir, sturdy enough to smash.

**Silicone spatula.** Perfect for mixing, folding, scraping, and dividing.

**Whisk.** One large classic whisk will do everything you need it to.

**Electric mixer.** A whisk can do everything an electric mixer can do, but whipping cream and egg whites sure is easier when you can give your arm a break! They're pretty inexpensive, too.

**Tongs.** Tongs are great for everything from flipping meat to lifting cooked spaghetti out of the water to rescuing runaway veggies from the stovetop. We prefer ones with silicone tips since they offer a no-slip grip on foods; plus, they won't scratch nonstick cookware.

**Can opener.** The classic cheap-and-cheerful hand-crank model still works best.

**Spider skimmer.** With a long handle and a sieve-like scoop, this is like a slotted spoon but so much more efficient. It's essential for removing fried foods from hot oil, and comes in handy for lifting everything from ravioli to baby potatoes from boiling water.

**Ladle.** Great for soups, obviously, but also perfect for dividing batter, making pancakes, and drizzling sauces.

**Instant-read thermometer.** Buy a digital one for quick reads on meat temperatures and to check if your oil is ready for frying.

**Rolling pin.** Roll out dough, crush ice, and turn graham crackers into crumbs. French pins made from a single tapered piece of wood are the easiest to use and most versatile variety.

**Microplane.** Zest citrus, finely grate cheese, and quickly grate ginger, garlic, and nutmeg.

**Vegetable peeler.** Peel apples and potatoes, shave ribbons of Parmesan, or make chocolate curls. Y-shaped and swivel styles work about the same, so pick your preference.

**Mixing bowls.** Find a stackable set of small, medium, and large bowls for easy storage. Stainless steel is the best for easy cleaning and storage and won't hold odors like plastic can. Small ramekins or glass prep bowls are also great to have on hand for prepping chopped ingredients and measuring out spices.

**Oven mitts and trivet.** Find a comfortable set of oven mitts and a trivet to protect your kitchen surfaces from hot pots and pans.

**Kitchen towels.** Decorative tea towels are wonderful, but kitchen towels (more absorbent and ecofriendly than paper towels) are the best for catching spills and cleaning up surfaces. In a pinch, you can use these to protect a surface from a hot pan as well.

**Food storage.** For packing lunches, storing leftovers, and freezing soups. Glass or silicone sets are great, but a cheap, reliable, and ecofriendly move is washing and saving takeout containers. (The round quart-size containers are storage gold.) If you plan on reheating food in the microwave in these containers, be sure you invest in BPA-free ones.

**Plastic wrap, foil, parchment paper, and silicone baking mats.** For all things storage and baking related. Save yourself the trouble of a smoke-filled kitchen and remember that parchment paper and waxed paper are NOT interchangeable!

**Ruler.** Keep a 24-inch metal ruler at the ready for kitchen-use only. It'll be essential for measuring rolled-out pastry, and also handy for evenly pushing up dough as you roll cinnamon rolls (page 30) or babka (page 19).

**Rimmed baking sheet.** Find a pan that's roughly 18 by 13 inches with a 1-inch rim (that's known as a half sheet pan). Go for a thick, sturdy pan that will hold its shape and evenly conduct heat for perfect browning every time. A smaller sheet pan is nice to have for toasting nuts or roasting smaller amounts of food, too.

**Large and small saucepans with lids.** For all the basics, from making rice to reheating leftovers. Do a little research before investing in a good set; ones with heavy bottoms are usually more reliable for conducting heat.

**Nonstick skillet.** Great for scrambled eggs, pancakes, and anything delicate that shouldn't be heavily seared. Don't invest a lot of money in a nonstick pan—they should be replaced as soon as the coating starts to wear/get scratched.

**Cast-iron skillet.** For getting a hard sear on meats and vegetables, and moving foods back and forth between the stovetop and the oven. Investing in a good 12-inch skillet (and taking care of it) will take your cooking over the top.

Cleaning a cast-iron skillet is the most important part of owning one. Use warm water and a pan brush to get the surface clean, and turn to a mixture of kosher salt and a few drops of any inexpensive neutral oil to scrub off any stuck-on bits. Soap can be your absolute last resort, but never use any abrasive sponges. After washing, place the skillet on a burner over high heat to dry it thoroughly, then remove it from the heat. Dab a paper towel with vegetable oil, then wipe the entire inside of the skillet to coat. Let cool completely before storing.

**Grill pan.** A cast-iron skillet will give food a great sear, but if you're craving grill marks—or need a deeper char without overcooking—a grill pan is worth the investment.

**Dutch oven.** Use it to make soups, boil pasta, and deep-fry. A 5- or 6-quart capacity will be just right.

**Blender and food processor.** Many brands make great multiuse blenders with food processor attachments. Save space (and money!) by getting a multipurpose machine that can do both.

**Rectangular baking pan (9 by 13 inches).** For making rolls, bars, and other treats.

**Square baking pan (8 by 8 inches).** Great for making brownies and other desserts but also cornbread and baked oatmeal.

**Loaf pan (9 by 5 inches).** Use it for baking bread and freezing homemade ice cream.

## The Unexpected

Not required, but a few cheap and easy-to-find tools can take anything over the top.

**Piping bags.** Not necessary (see page 35), but a sure way to cleanly pipe pastry dough and decorations. They're often sold in kits with a variety of fun tips. In a pinch, you can also use a small resealable plastic bag with one of the bottom corners snipped off.

**Ice cube trays.** These come in a variety of shapes to make unique ice cubes (see tips on page 143) that can perk up even a simple glass of seltzer.

**Cookie cutters.** Larger ones are fun for cutting biscuit shapes (and cookie dough, obviously!); mini cutters in shapes like stars are great for cutting decorative designs out of fruit like pineapple and watermelon.

**Flames.** Sparklers in classic and rainbow colors, plus birthday candles in all sizes and colors, instantly make any dish an event. Just make sure you're in a ventilated area before lighting them so fire alarms don't join the party.

**Picks.** Cocktail umbrellas, decorative toothpicks, and flamingo, pineapple, and palm tree picks are all great for serious vacation vibes.

**Straws.** Crazy-loop straws, striped paper straws, and tamarind straws will make all your drinks irresistible.

**Glow.** Light-up ice cubes, color-changing spoons, and glow sticks in a variety of shapes lend an instant over-the-top touch.

**Edible luster spray.** Even though it's edible (and so fun!), it has an odd taste that doesn't always complement the dish. Instead of spraying it on food, we prefer to use it to spray the outside of glasses or serving trays to give them extra shimmer.

# over the top
## OF THE MORNING

# rainbow unicorn BABKA

MAKES 1 LOAF

Rainbows and cereal and sprinkles and icing: The only way this babka could be more over the top is if it were delivered by an actual unicorn. Matcha and pitaya powders (see page 11) create two color-saturated doughs, while a ton of fruity cereal adds pops of color and crunch. A multicolored icing made from butterfly pea tea creates pools of blue and purple. Then comes a final dusting of glistening sugar sprinkles and, well, breakfast just can't get any more magical.

**1** **Make the babka:** In a small skillet, melt 4 tablespoons (½ stick) of the butter over low heat, then remove the skillet from the heat. Whisk in the milk and sugar. Sprinkle the yeast over the mixture and set aside for about 10 minutes, until the yeast is cloudy and fragrant.

**2** Set two medium bowls on a work surface. To each bowl, add 1 egg, ½ teaspoon of the salt, and 1½ cups of the flour. Add the matcha to one bowl and the pitaya to the other bowl. Pour ½ cup of the yeast mixture into the matcha bowl and the remaining yeast mixture into the pitaya bowl. Use a wooden spoon to stir the matcha mixture, then use clean hands to knead the dough to fully incorporate the flour. Add 1 to 2 tablespoons more flour as needed to form a cohesive, slightly sticky dough. Repeat with the pitaya mixture. Cover each bowl with plastic wrap and let rest for 30 minutes.

**3** Preheat the oven to 350°F and set a rack in the center. Coat a 9 by 5-inch loaf pan with nonstick spray. Fold a 12 by 10-inch piece of parchment paper in half, then lay it across the width of the pan to create two overhanging flaps. Coat the parchment with nonstick spray.

*recipe continues*

## For the Babka

6 tablespoons (¾ stick) unsalted butter

½ cup whole milk

¼ cup sugar

1 (¼-ounce) packet active dry yeast (2¼ teaspoons)

2 large eggs

1 teaspoon kosher salt

3 cups all-purpose flour, plus more as needed

2 tablespoons sweetened matcha powder (see note, page 11)

1 tablespoon pitaya powder (see note, page 11)

Nonstick cooking spray

1 cup fruity crisp rice cereal

## For the Icing

2 tablespoons whole milk

1 tablespoon butterfly pea flower tea (see page 11)

1 cup powdered sugar

½ teaspoon fresh lemon juice

Colored sanding sugar, for serving

**4** On a lightly floured work surface, roll out the matcha dough into a 6 by 12-inch rectangle, about ¼ inch thick. Repeat with the pitaya dough. Arrange the rectangles of dough side-by-side and pinch the middle edges together to join them, creating a 12-inch square.

**5** In a small microwave-safe bowl, microwave the remaining 2 tablespoons butter on high for about 30 seconds, until melted. Brush the melted butter all over the dough. Sprinkle the cereal evenly over the dough and press down to set the cereal in the dough.

**6** Starting from the matcha edge of the square, roll the dough tightly into a cylinder. Use a paring knife to slice the cylinder in half lengthwise to expose the layers inside. With the cut sides of the two ropes of dough facing out, twist the ropes around each other. Pinch the top and bottom edges to seal, then carefully transfer the twist of dough to the prepared pan.

**7** Bake for about 45 minutes, until the dough is golden brown on top and a skewer or toothpick inserted into the center comes out clean. Remove from the oven and let cool in the pan until cool enough to handle, about 1 hour.

**8** **Meanwhile, make the icing:** While the babka is cooling, in a small microwave-safe bowl, microwave the milk for about 15 seconds, until hot. Stir in the tea and set aside to steep for about 1 hour.

**9** Set two small bowls on a work surface. Scoop out the tea and discard, then pour 1 tablespoon of the infused milk into each of the bowls. Add ½ cup of the powdered sugar to each bowl. Whisk to thoroughly combine. Add the lemon juice to one of the bowls and whisk; the icing will turn purple. (Don't add lemon juice or return the whisk to the other bowl; you want this icing to stay blue.)

**10** Use the overhanging parchment to lift the loaf out of the pan and set it on a serving tray. Discard the parchment. Spoon the blue icing all over the loaf. Repeat with the purple icing. Top with sprinkles and serve immediately.

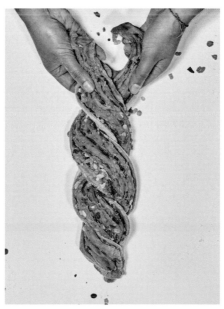

# AVOCADO *benedict*

**For the Benedict**

2 tablespoons (packed) light brown sugar

2 tablespoons pineapple juice

1 teaspoon Dijon mustard

4 slices Canadian bacon

2 large avocados

Kosher salt

4 large eggs

2 English muffins, split

2 tablespoons unsalted butter, cut into 4 pieces

**For the Hollandaise**

½ cup (1 stick) unsalted butter

3 large egg yolks

1 tablespoon fresh lemon juice

½ teaspoon kosher salt

Minced fresh chives and cayenne pepper, for serving

How do you take a classic and make it even *better?* Add an avocado! We took this famous brunch must-order and pushed it over the top by baking the egg until perfectly runny *in* an avocado half! A buttered English muffin and sweet pineapple—brown sugar glazed slices of Canadian bacon go into the oven alongside the egg while it bakes; as the butter melts in the oven, it pools into the nooks and crannies of the English muffin—brilliant, right? Meanwhile, you're whipping up an easy hollandaise sauce in the blender. A breakfast that is arguably as simple as it is impressive, and different enough to feel fun and fresh, too.

**1 Make the Benedict:** Preheat the oven to 400°F and set a rack in the center. Line a rimmed baking sheet with a silicone baking mat or parchment paper.

**2** In a small bowl, whisk together the brown sugar, pineapple juice, and mustard. Add the Canadian bacon and set aside to marinate.

**3** Slice the avocados in half and remove the pits. Peel the skin from the avocado halves and season the flesh with plenty of salt. Set the avocado halves cut-side up on the prepared baking sheet and crack 1 egg into the well in the center of each. Sprinkle salt over each egg.

**4** Bake the avocado halves for about 6 minutes, until the egg whites have just begun to set. Remove the baking sheet from the oven and add the English muffin halves, cut-side up. Place a piece of butter on each one. Remove the Canadian bacon from the marinade and arrange the pieces on the baking sheet. Return the baking sheet to the oven and bake for about 7 minutes, until the egg whites are set, the muffins are toasted, and the bacon is browned.

**5** **Meanwhile, make the hollandaise:** In a small skillet, melt the butter over low heat. Once the butter is melted, combine the egg yolks, lemon juice, and salt in a blender. Blend on low for about 15 seconds, until smooth. With the blender on low, remove the lid and very slowly stream in the melted butter, then continue blending on low until the butter is fully incorporated and the sauce is thick, about 30 seconds more.

**6** Divide the English muffin halves among four plates. Arrange a piece of bacon on top of each, then invert an avocado half so the egg is on top of the bacon. Spoon the hollandaise over each avocado half and garnish with chives and cayenne pepper as desired. Serve immediately.

# POTATO CHIP *omelet*

A whole bag of chips in an omelet?!! "Crazy," you'll say. A potato chip salad on top?? "I'm done!" you'll scream. One bite in? "It's the chips for me," you'll concede. Somehow, through chemistry or witchcraft or something, the chips in the omelet swell into perfect potato-y bites, while the chips on top provide a delicious savory crunch. Junk food has never felt so elegant!

**1** Preheat the oven to 400°F and set a rack in the center.

**2** In a large skillet, fry the bacon over medium heat for about 5 minutes on each side, until the fat has rendered and the bacon is crisp.

**3** While the bacon cooks, whisk together the eggs and salt in a large bowl. Measure 2 cups of chips and set aside in a medium bowl. Add the remaining chips to the bowl with the eggs. Use a spatula to crush the chips and fold them into the eggs until the chips are coated with egg.

**4** Transfer the bacon to paper towels to drain. Pour the egg mixture into the bacon fat in the skillet, using a silicone spatula to smooth the chips so they're fully submerged in the egg. Cook over medium heat for about 4 minutes, until the bottom and sides of the omelet are set. Transfer the skillet to the oven and bake for about 10 minutes, until the top is starting to brown and the center is set.

**5** Meanwhile, crush the remaining chips in the medium bowl into small pieces. Add the parsley and chives and toss to combine. In a separate medium bowl, combine the arugula, vinegar, and oil and toss to combine. Slice the bacon in half lengthwise, then chop it into small pieces.

**6** Remove the omelet from the oven and slide it onto a serving plate. Arrange the arugula mixture on top of the omelet, then sprinkle the chip mixture over the arugula. Sprinkle the bacon on top of the chips, then slice and serve immediately.

## SERVES 4

2 slices thick-cut bacon

12 large eggs

1 teaspoon kosher salt

1 (12½-ounce) bag sour cream and onion potato chips

1 tablespoon finely chopped fresh parsley

1 tablespoon finely chopped fresh chives

2 cups arugula

2 tablespoons white wine vinegar

1 tablespoon olive oil

# BREAKFAST NACHO
## biscuits

SERVES 8

¼ cup red wine vinegar

1 teaspoon sugar

1 teaspoon plus ½ teaspoon kosher salt

½ red onion, thinly sliced

1 (16-ounce) tube store-bought flaky biscuits

1 tablespoon olive oil

2 fresh (Mexican) chorizo links, casings removed

8 large eggs

¼ teaspoon freshly ground black pepper

12 slices yellow American cheese

½ cup whole milk

1 (4-ounce) can green chiles

1 (15.5-ounce) can black beans, drained and rinsed

1 avocado, halved, pitted, peeled, and thinly sliced

½ cup fresh cilantro leaves

Okay, so imagine biscuits and gravy. Got it? But the biscuits are those guilty-pleasure, how-are-these-so-buttery, slightly-stressful-popping-the-can ones that are somehow insanely good. Then they're sliced in half and toasted a little on the insides. And the gravy is a spicy cheese sauce with chorizo. Toss on some scrambled eggs, black beans, and avocado, and suddenly you have breakfast nachos. An iconic mash-up of two morning delights!

**1** In a medium bowl, whisk together the vinegar, sugar, 1 teaspoon of the salt, and ¼ cup warm water. Add the onion and toss to coat. Set aside.

**2** Open the tube of biscuits, separate them, and place them on a rimmed baking sheet. Bake according to the package directions.

**3** While the biscuits bake, in a large nonstick skillet, heat the oil over medium heat. When the oil is shimmering, add the chorizo. Cook, stirring and breaking up the meat with a wooden spoon, for about 5 minutes, until browned. Meanwhile, crack the eggs into a medium bowl, add the remaining ½ teaspoon salt and the pepper, and whisk together.

**4** Transfer the chorizo to a small bowl, leaving the oil in the skillet. Add the eggs to the skillet and cook over medium heat, stirring continuously, for about 5 minutes, until the eggs are slightly set but still runny. Remove the skillet from the heat and let the eggs finish cooking in the residual heat from the pan.

**5** In a small saucepan, combine the cheese, milk, and green chiles. Heat over low heat, whisking occasionally, for about 5 minutes, until the cheese is fully melted and the sauce is smooth. Stir in the chorizo.

**6** Remove the biscuits from the oven and let cool slightly (keep the oven on). Slice the baked biscuits in half and arrange them cut-side up on the baking sheet. Return the biscuits to the oven for about 5 minutes, until lightly toasted.

**7** Spoon the black beans over each biscuit half on the baking sheet, followed by the eggs. Drizzle the chorizo cheese sauce over everything and top with the avocado slices. Drain the pickled red onion and garnish everything with the onion and cilantro. Serve immediately.

# ELVIS *waffles*

2 slices thick-cut bacon, halved crosswise

4 bananas

¾ cup creamy peanut butter

½ cup sugar

2 large eggs

2 teaspoons baking soda

1 teaspoon kosher salt

1 teaspoon vanilla extract

1½ cups whole milk

2 cups all-purpose flour

¼ cup honey

Elvis Presley's favorite sandwich was a peanut butter, banana, and bacon sandwich fried in bacon fat (*yes, King*). To take it truly over the top, why not mash the banana and peanut butter into the waffle batter, griddle the waffles in bacon fat, and top them with crispy bacon bits, more bananas, and a peanut butter–honey drizzle? Breakfast has left the building.

**1** Preheat the oven to 300°F and set a rack in the center. Set a standard waffle iron to medium heat.

**2** Arrange the bacon in a small skillet and cook over medium heat for about 5 minutes on each side, until the fat has rendered and the bacon is crisp. Transfer the bacon to paper towels to drain, reserving the fat in the skillet. Remove the skillet from the heat and set aside.

**3** Use a fork to mash 2 of the bananas in a large bowl. Add ½ cup of the peanut butter, the sugar, eggs, baking soda, salt, and vanilla and whisk until the eggs are incorporated and the mixture is smooth. Add the milk and flour and whisk until the batter is combined.

**4** Brush the waffle iron with the reserved bacon fat. Use a ladle to spoon the batter into the waffle iron, being careful not to overfill it, and cook according to the manufacturer's instructions. Transfer the waffle to a rimmed baking sheet and keep warm in the oven while you cook the remaining batter.

**5** While the waffles cook, prep the toppings. In a small microwave-safe bowl, microwave the remaining ¼ cup peanut butter on high for 15 to 30 seconds, until the peanut butter is loose and warm. Stir in the honey. Slice the remaining 2 bananas. Chop the bacon into small pieces.

**6** Stack the waffles on a plate or serving platter and top with the banana slices, bacon pieces, and peanut butter–honey. Serve immediately.

# PUMPKIN SPICE LATTE

 **MAKES 9 ROLLS**

### For the Dough

4 tablespoons (½ stick)
unsalted butter

1 cup whole milk

1 tablespoon granulated
sugar

1 (¼-ounce) packet active dry
yeast (2¼ teaspoons)

1 large egg

1½ teaspoons kosher salt

1 teaspoon baking powder

3½ cups all-purpose flour,
plus more for dusting

Nonstick cooking spray

### For the Filling

½ cup (1 stick) unsalted
butter

1 cup (packed) light brown
sugar

½ cup pumpkin pie spice

### For the Icing

3 tablespoons whole milk

1 teaspoon instant coffee

2 cups powdered sugar

Every fall (but actually late summer at this point), pumpkin spice takes over everything: coffee, cereal, beer, even canned meats. So why fight the feeling? A blend of warm spices—pumpkin pie spices, to be exact (seriously, that's how the spice blend is labeled!)—transform cinnamon rolls into an extra-cozy breakfast treat. And a latte glaze made from milk and coffee eases into all the crevices, soaking into their very core. Why worry about being basic when this is basically incredible?

**1** **Make the dough:** In a small skillet, melt the butter over low heat, then remove the skillet from the heat and add the milk. Set aside to warm the milk slightly.

**2** In a large bowl, whisk together the granulated sugar, yeast, egg, salt, and baking powder. Add the flour and the milk mixture. Use a wooden spoon to stir until a smooth dough forms. Cover the bowl with plastic wrap and set it in a warm place to rise for 1 hour, until the dough has doubled in size and a finger pressed into the dough leaves an indent. Punch down the dough with your hands, then cover the bowl again and let rest in the refrigerator for 30 minutes.

**3** **Make the filling:** In a medium microwave-safe bowl, microwave the butter on high until melted, about 45 seconds. Stir in the brown sugar and pumpkin pie spice to create a soft paste.

**4** Coat a 9 by 13-inch baking pan with nonstick spray. Turn the dough out onto a lightly floured surface and roll it into an 18 by 12-inch rectangle, about ¼ inch thick. Use a silicone spatula to spread the filling over the dough, leaving a ½-inch border.

**5** Starting with the long (18-inch) side of the rectangle closest to you, begin to loosely roll up the dough around the filling, starting in the center and working out to the ends. Once the roll is complete, gently pinch the seam to seal. Slice the dough crosswise into 9 equal rolls and transfer them to the prepared baking pan, cut-side up, leaving plenty of room between each roll. Cover the pan with plastic wrap and set it in a warm place to rise for 1 hour, until the rolls have doubled in size.

**6** Meanwhile, preheat the oven to 350°F and set a rack in the center.

**7** Bake the rolls for 30 to 35 minutes, until they are golden brown and firm. Remove from the oven and let cool in the pan for 10 minutes.

**8** **Meanwhile, make the icing:** In a medium microwave-safe bowl, microwave the milk on high for 15 seconds, until steaming. Add the instant coffee and whisk to dissolve. (Alternatively, use 3 tablespoons strong brewed coffee or espresso in place of the milk and instant coffee.) Whisk in the powdered sugar until the frosting is smooth and falls in thick ribbons from the whisk.

**9** Spoon the frosting over the warm rolls and serve immediately.

# dulce de leche– stuffed FRENCH TOAST

**SERVES 2**

1 (1-pound) brioche loaf

6 tablespoons store-bought dulce de leche

1 tablespoon unsalted butter

3 large eggs

1½ cups whole milk

3 tablespoons (packed) light brown sugar

½ teaspoon kosher salt

Powdered sugar, whipped cream, sprinkles, and butterscotch chips, for serving

This is a breakfast of pure indulgence. Brioche, an enriched bread made with lots of eggs and butter—essentially the most elegant loaf of bread around—is sliced thick and then stuffed with dulce de leche, which roughly translates to "caramel, but better." Then the whole affair is fried in butter and blanketed in sugar, cream, and sprinkles. It's French toast doing the absolute most.

**1** Slice the brioche in half crosswise, then slice each half in half again to create 4 thick, equal-size pieces. Cut a 2-inch-long slit in the bottom of each piece of bread, cutting all the way into— but not through—the bread to create a deep pocket for filling.

**2** Working with one piece at a time, squeeze the sides of the bread to open the pocket and spoon in 1½ tablespoons of dulce de leche. Repeat with the remaining bread and dulce de leche.

**3** In a medium skillet, melt the butter over medium heat until it starts to bubble slightly.

**4** Meanwhile, in a large, shallow bowl, whisk together the eggs, milk, brown sugar, and salt. Place 2 pieces of the stuffed bread in the egg mixture and soak for about 30 seconds on each side. Transfer to the skillet and cook for about 2 minutes on each side, until golden brown and crisp. Transfer the French toast to a plate and repeat with the remaining pieces of bread.

**5** Stack the French toast on a serving plate. Top with powdered sugar, whipped cream, sprinkles, and butterscotch chips. Serve immediately.

# BERRY
## baked oatmeal

Do you want a healthy breakfast or an indulgent one? This baked oatmeal combines the best of both into one. The base is a nourishing and satisfying baked oatmeal loaded with berries. But then, party time: The whole thing is topped with crumbled toaster pastries. The best part of being over the top is adding a little celebration to the day.

**SERVES 9**

Nonstick cooking spray

2 large eggs

2 cups rolled oats

1 cup whole milk

1 cup (packed) light brown sugar

1 teaspoon ground cinnamon

1 teaspoon baking powder

1 teaspoon kosher salt

2 cups frozen mixed berries

4 frosted strawberry toaster pastries, crumbled

Pure maple syrup or fruit syrup, for serving

**1** Preheat the oven to 350°F and set a rack in the center. Lightly coat an 8-inch square baking dish with nonstick spray.

**2** In a large bowl, lightly whisk the eggs. Add the oats, milk, brown sugar, cinnamon, baking powder, and salt and whisk to combine. Use a spatula to fold in the frozen berries, then transfer the oatmeal to the prepared baking dish.

**3** Bake for about 45 minutes, until the oatmeal has risen and is slightly firm. Remove the baking dish from the oven and sprinkle the crumbled toaster pastries over the top, then bake for 15 minutes more, until the oatmeal is fully set and the toaster pastry topping is toasted. Let cool completely in the pan, about 1 hour. Slice into 9 pieces, then serve. Drizzle with maple or fruit syrup as desired.

# peanut butter & jelly DONUTS

MAKES
8 DONUTS

If you're a PB&J lover, prepare for the best day of your life. These dead-simple donuts (pop a can of biscuit dough and you're halfway there) get fried and then filled with jelly and covered in a peanut butter glaze. This recipe makes 8 donuts—the serving size is up to you.

**1 Make the donuts:** In a Dutch oven, heat the oil over medium-high heat until it reaches 350°F on an instant-read thermometer.

**2** While the oil heats, remove the biscuits from the tube and press each biscuit to flatten it slightly to about 3¼ inches in diameter and ½ inch thick. Once the oil reaches 350°F, add a few biscuits to the pot (you don't want it to be overcrowded) and fry for about 2 minutes on each side, until deep golden brown. Transfer the donuts to a wire rack and let cool slightly. Repeat with the remaining biscuits, letting the oil return to 350°F between batches and adjusting the heat as needed while frying to maintain the oil temperature.

**3** When the donuts are cool enough to handle, pour the jelly into a piping bag fitted with a small circular tip (or see Note). Use a paring knife to cut a small hole in the side of each donut, then pipe about 2 tablespoons of the jelly into each.

**4 Make the glaze:** In a medium bowl, whisk together the milk, peanut butter, and powdered sugar to create a soft but thick glaze. Add 1 tablespoon more of milk if the glaze is too thick.

**5** Dip the top of each donut into the glaze to coat. Garnish with peanuts and sprinkles, as desired, and serve immediately.

### For the Donuts

4 cups vegetable oil

1 (16-ounce) tube store-bought flaky biscuits

1 cup fruit jelly (any flavor)

### For the Glaze

¼ cup whole milk, plus more as needed

½ cup creamy peanut butter

½ cup powdered sugar

Chopped peanuts and sprinkles

### NOTE

A homemade piping bag can be as simple as using a zip-top bag with the corner snipped off. But if you need the sturdiness of a tip—for filling donuts or piping pastry dough—just grab a gallon-size zip-top bag, duct tape, and scissors. Fold the bag into a sharp triangle. Cut a long piece of duct tape the length of the seam, including the tip, and use it to seal the seam. Place the bag in a tall drinking glass with the edges folded over the top of the glass, then fill it with whatever you'll be piping. Squeeze out any excess air, seal the top, and snip the tip. You're ready to pipe and fill with ease!

# CHEEZ-IT *quiche*

### For the Crust

Nonstick cooking spray

6½ cups baked cheese crackers, such as Cheez-Its (from one 21-ounce box)

4 tablespoons (½ stick) unsalted butter, melted

2 large eggs

### For the Filling

4 large eggs

¾ cup heavy cream

½ teaspoon kosher salt

¼ teaspoon freshly ground black pepper

2 cups thawed frozen broccoli florets, cut into bite-size pieces

1 cup grated cheddar cheese

A crust made of crackers is nothing new (see: grahams, saltines) but making one from Cheez-Its? Well, that's a revelation. The cheese actually complements, rather than overpowers, a simple broccoli cheddar quiche. And the crushed crackers form a perfect crust, dense but not hard, plus a crunchy coating for the top. Weird on paper, delicious on the plate.

**1 Make the crust:** Preheat the oven to 375°F and set a rack in the center. Coat a 9-inch pie plate with nonstick spray.

**2** Pulse the cheese crackers in a food processor about 8 times, until broken down into small crumbs. In a large bowl, whisk together the melted butter and eggs until smooth. Add 4 cups of the cracker crumbs and toss to fully coat. Transfer the remaining ½ cup cracker crumbs to a small bowl and set aside.

**3** Pour the cracker mixture into the prepared pie plate and press into an even layer over the bottom and about halfway up the side of the plate. Prick the crust with a fork along the bottom and sides. Bake for about 12 minutes, until the crust is toasted and fragrant.

**4 Meanwhile, make the filling:** In a medium bowl, whisk together the eggs, cream, salt, and pepper. Fold in the broccoli and cheese.

**5** Pour the filling into the crust and bake for 10 minutes. Sprinkle the top with the reserved cracker crumbs and bake for about 10 minutes more, until the center of the quiche is set. Let cool for about 30 minutes before slicing and serving.

# TRIPLE-DECKER
## breakfast
## sandwich

MAKES 2 SANDWICHES

Egg and cheese or avocado toast? Why choose! Load up on breakfast in the best way possible with layer after layer (after layer) of the good stuff. The base is a bagel half, topped with a sausage patty *and* bacon strips, then covered in melted cheese. Round 2 is an egg fried in the middle of a bagel. And round 3 is more bagel with mashed avocado that's sprinkled with everything bagel seasoning, naturally. Mash it down and take a big bite, or dive in with a fork and knife. There is no wrong way to attack this monster.

2 slices thick-cut bacon, halved crosswise

2 sausage patties

2 slices American cheese

4 everything bagels

2 large eggs

1 medium avocado, halved and pitted

Hot sauce and everything bagel seasoning, for serving

**1** Arrange the bacon and sausage patties in a large skillet and cook over medium heat for about 5 minutes on each side, until the sausage is browned and the bacon is crisp. Place 2 pieces of bacon on each sausage patty and place a slice of cheese on top. Transfer the patty stacks to a plate and set aside; reserve the fat in the skillet.

**2** Cut 2 of the bagels in half and place them to the skillet, cut-side down, pressing on them so they soak up the fat in the pan Cook over medium heat for about 2 minutes, until toasted and browned to your liking. Transfer to a plate and set aside. (If all 4 bagel halves don't fit at once, brush the fat over the cut side of each slice, then toast them two at a time until browned.)

**3** Cut the remaining 2 bagels in half and place just the bottom halves in the skillet, cut-side down, pressing on them so they soak up the fat (freeze the tops for another day). Crack an egg into the hole in each bagel and fry for about 2 minutes, until the bagel is toasted and the egg whites have begun to set. Flip the bagels and cook for about 2 minutes more, until the whites have fully set. Transfer the egg-filled bagels to the plate with the other bagel halves.

**4** Scoop the flesh from the avocado into a small bowl and use a fork to mash it. Spread the mashed avocado over the cut side of each toasted bagel top. Arrange the sausage patty stacks on the toasted bagel bottoms. Place an egg-filled bagel on each patty stack. Drizzle some hot sauce over the eggs. Sprinkle everything bagel seasoning over the avocado and set on top of the eggs. Place each sandwich on a plate, cut in half with a sharp knife, and serve immediately.

# chia pudding PARFAIT

1 cup chia seeds

3 cups unsweetened plain almond milk

1 tablespoon vanilla extract

3 tablespoons sugar

1 (0.73-ounce) packet hot chocolate mix

¼ teaspoon unsweetened strawberry drink mix, such as Kool-Aid (from one 0.14-ounce packet)

12 chocolate sandwich cookies

24 vanilla wafers

12 fresh strawberries, trimmed and thinly sliced

Stir together chia seeds and milk (dairy-free or cow, whatever moves you), leave it overnight in the fridge, and top with fresh fruit and granola the next morning for a healthy and super-tasty breakfast pudding. Okay, now that we have the ground rules, let's amp it up. This Neapolitan ice cream—inspired parfait uses hot cocoa mix and strawberry drink mix to color and flavor the pudding. Then just layer the vanilla, chocolate, and strawberry mixtures with delicious fillings (namely, cookies and strawberries) to add exciting textures. Healthy or over the top, it's up to you.

**1** Divide the chia seeds and almond milk evenly among three medium bowls. Whisk well to combine.

**2** To the first bowl, add the vanilla and 2 tablespoons of the sugar and whisk to combine. To the second bowl, add the hot chocolate mix and whisk to combine. To the third bowl, add ¼ teaspoon of the strawberry drink mix and the remaining 1 tablespoon sugar and whisk to combine. Cover the bowls tightly with plastic wrap and refrigerate overnight.

**3** Crumble the chocolate sandwich cookies and divide them among four serving glasses. Scoop ¼ cup of the chocolate chia mixture over the cookies in each glass. Crumble the vanilla wafers and divide them among the glasses, then scoop ¼ cup of the vanilla chia mixture over the wafers. Fan the strawberries over the vanilla chia in each glass, then top with ¼ cup of the strawberry chia mixture as the final layer. Serve immediately. (Alternatively, the chia puddings can be stored, covered, in the fridge for up to 1 week and used to assemble individual parfaits as needed.)

# HOMEMADE
## cookie cereal

What is cuter than a bowl full of tiny cookies? Nothing! In the grand tradition of breakfast for dinner, we present dessert for breakfast. This is a perfect recipe to make with friends, creating an assembly line of dough balls on baking sheets. Go for the four flavors in this recipe, or pick one and commit to it. Either way, it's a sweet treat.

½ cup (1 stick) unsalted butter, melted

¾ cup (packed) light brown sugar

¼ cup granulated sugar

1 large egg

1 teaspoon vanilla extract

½ teaspoon baking soda

½ teaspoon kosher salt

1¾ cups all-purpose flour

2 tablespoons smooth peanut butter

2 tablespoons peanut butter chips

2 tablespoons unsweetened cocoa powder

2 tablespoons white chocolate chips

2 tablespoons mini M&M's

2 tablespoons semisweet chocolate chips

2 large egg whites

Milk of choice, for serving

**1** Preheat the oven to 350°F and set a rack in the center. Line two rimmed baking sheets with silicone baking mats or parchment paper.

**2** In a large bowl, whisk together the melted butter and both sugars until a thick paste forms. Add the egg, vanilla, baking soda, and salt and whisk until combined. Add the flour and use a wooden spoon to stir until a cohesive dough forms and no flour streaks remain.

**3** Divide the dough evenly among four bowls (about ½ cup of dough per bowl). In the first bowl, fold in the peanut butter and peanut butter chips. In the second bowl, fold in the cocoa powder and white chocolate chips. In the third bowl, fold in the M&M's. In the fourth bowl, fold in the semisweet chocolate chips.

**4** In a small bowl, whisk the egg whites to combine. Use a ½-teaspoon measure to scoop out and roll the dough into balls (about 5 grams each). Dip the dough balls in the egg whites and place them on one of the prepared baking sheets, lining up about 40 balls of dough and leaving about 1 inch between each ball. Bake for 10 minutes, rotating the pan halfway through, until the cookies have cracked and slightly spread. Let cool completely on the baking sheet before transferring to an airtight container.

**5** While the first batch of cookies bakes, repeat to fill the second prepared baking sheet. Continue to work in batches, letting the baking sheets cool between each batch. You should have about 120 cookies by the end.

**6** The cookie cereal can be stored in the airtight container at room temperature for up to 1 week. For those who can't wait, pour some into a big bowl, top with milk, and dive in!

# out to LUNCH

# HOT DIGGITY *dog*

These dogs run the gamut from no way! to NO WAY!, but they're all absolutely delicious. Each recipe makes one hot dog, so whip up a couple for lunch or make multiples of each to feed a crowd. For an over-the-top barbecue or game-day tailgating party, set out stations with all the different toppings for an interactive, make-your-own-hot-dog lunch. The possibilities are endless!

## THE CHIP DOG

1 hot dog bun

1 cooked hot dog or veggie dog

Crushed mustard-, dill-, and ketchup-flavored potato chips, for serving

Place the bun on a plate and put the hot dog inside. Top with the crushed chips. Serve immediately.

## THE BIG CHEESE

1 hot dog bun

1 cooked hot dog or veggie dog

Baked cheese crackers, cheese puffs, cheese sandwich crackers, fish-shaped cheese crackers, and/or spray cheese, for serving

Place the bun on a plate and add the hot dog. Top with the baked cheese crackers, cheese puffs, cheese sandwich crackers, fish-shaped cheese crackers, and spray cheese. Serve immediately.

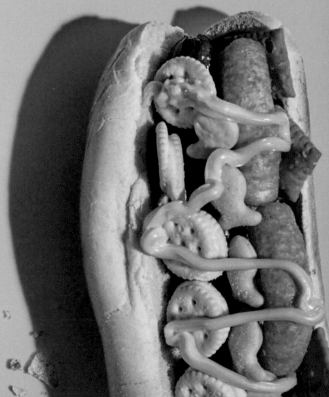

## THE CHILI CHEESE DOG

1 hot dog or veggie dog, finely diced

2 tablespoons diced jalapeño

½ cup chunky salsa

¼ teaspoon garlic powder

1 large piece cornbread (about 3 by 4 inches)

2 slices American cheese

Sliced scallions, for serving

**1** In a small saucepan, combine the hot dog, jalapeño, salsa, and garlic powder and bring to a simmer over medium heat. Cover, reduce the heat to low, and simmer for 10 minutes, until warmed through.

**2** Place the cornbread on a plate and cut a 1-inch-wide piece from the center. Stack the cheese slices and roll them into a thick cylinder, about the shape of a hot dog. Place the cheese in the cornbread cutout. Spoon the hot chili over the top and finish with scallions. Serve immediately, with a fork and knife.

## THE NEW YAWKER

2 tablespoons mayonnaise

2 tablespoons plain Greek yogurt

1 teaspoon white wine vinegar

¼ teaspoon garlic powder

¼ teaspoon sugar

⅛ cup shredded iceberg lettuce

2 tablespoons shredded red cabbage

2 tablespoons diced tomatoes

1 pretzel roll, sliced across the top

1 cooked hot dog or veggie dog

Chopped candied peanuts and crushed bagel chips, for topping.

**1** In a small bowl, whisk together the mayonnaise, yogurt, vinegar, garlic powder, and sugar. Add the lettuce, cabbage, and tomatoes and toss the slaw to combine.

**2** Place the pretzel roll on a plate and add the hot dog. Top with the slaw and finish with the peanuts and bagel chips. Serve immediately.

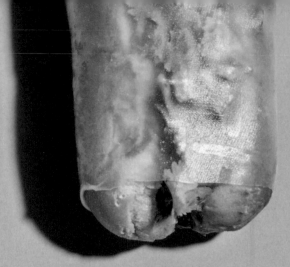

## THE THAI HOT DOG

¼ cup creamy peanut butter

2 tablespoons green curry paste

Juice of 1 lime

1 hot dog bun

1 tablespoon unsalted butter, at room temperature

1 rice paper wrapper

1 cooked hot dog or veggie dog

1 sprig of cilantro

2 fresh basil leaves

4 fresh mint leaves

1 tablespoon store-bought crispy fried onions

1 tablespoon chopped roasted, salted peanuts

**1** In a small bowl, whisk together the peanut butter, curry paste, and lime juice.

**2** Heat a small skillet over medium heat. Spread both sides of the hot dog bun with the butter. Toast the bun in the skillet for about 4 minutes, flipping halfway, until golden and toasted on both sides.

**3** Run the rice paper under warm water for a few seconds to moisten it, then spread it on a work surface. Place the toasted bun in the center and spread half the curry mixture inside the bun. Place the hot dog inside the bun and top with the cilantro, basil, mint, fried onions, and peanuts. Tuck the ends in, like a burrito, and tightly wrap the rice paper over the entire bun, pressing the edge together to seal. Serve immediately, with the remaining curry sauce for dipping.

## THE ICE CREAM "DOG"

¼ cup strawberry ice cream, at room temperature

2 cream-filled snack cakes

1 red candy lace

1 yellow candy lace

1 green candy lace, diced

**1** Place a piece of plastic wrap on a work surface. Scoop the ice cream into the center, then roll the plastic around the ice cream and gently roll the ice cream into a 4-inch cylinder (about the thickness of a hot dog). Twist the ends of the plastic to hold the ice cream in place. Freeze for 15 minutes.

**2** Set the snack cakes on a plate. Unwrap the ice cream and set it between the cakes. Top the ice cream with the red and yellow laces, forming them into snaky shapes to mimic squiggles of ketchup and mustard. Sprinkle with the green lace to mimic relish. Serve immediately.

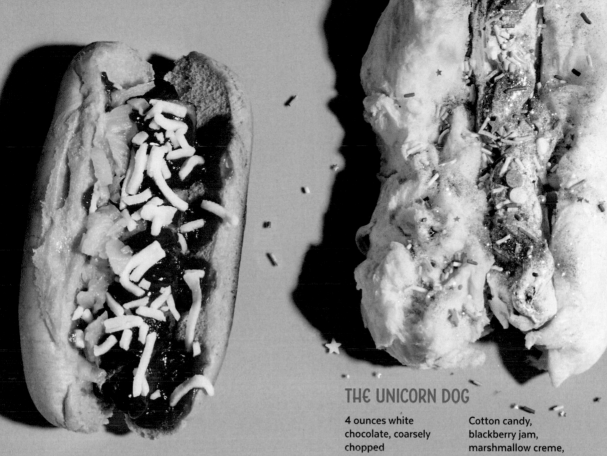

## THE UNICORN DOG

4 ounces white chocolate, coarsely chopped

1 frozen peeled banana

Cotton candy, blackberry jam, marshmallow creme, sprinkles, and edible glitter, for serving

**1** In a medium microwave-safe bowl, microwave the white chocolate on high for about 30 seconds, stirring every 10 seconds, until melted.

**2** Place the frozen banana on a plate lined with a small piece of parchment paper. Pour the melted white chocolate over the banana and freeze for 10 minutes to set the chocolate.

**3** Set 2 big pieces of cotton candy on a plate. Remove the chocolate-coated banana from the parchment and place it between the cotton candy pieces. Spoon or pipe jam and marshmallow creme on top of the banana. Garnish everything with sprinkles and glitter. Serve immediately.

## THE HAWAIIAN DOG

1 hot dog or veggie dog

1 slice thick-cut bacon (optional)

1 hot dog bun

Ketchup, drained crushed pineapple, and shredded mozzarella, for serving

**1** Heat a small skillet over medium heat. Starting at the bottom of the hot dog, wrap the bacon (if using) around the hot dog in a kind of spiral (use toothpicks to secure the ends if needed). Cook the hot dog in the skillet, turning to cook on all sides, for about 6 minutes, until the bacon is crisp and browned and the hot dog is warmed through.

**2** Place the bun on a plate and place the hot dog inside. Top with ketchup, pineapple, and mozzarella. Serve immediately.

# CALI-STYLE
## sushi burrito  MAKES 2 BURRITOS

All the handheld convenience of a burrito meets all the good feeling of sushi rolls. The tuna roll is served Cali-style (with French fries!) and the veggie roll also ups the game (with fried avocado!). Both of them get slathered in a trio of delicious sauces—sriracha mayo, wasabi mayo, and ginger tamari—then rolled like a burrito for a lunch on the go.

## TUNA ROLL

½ cup vegetable oil

1 cup frozen French fries, thawed

2 sheets nori

1 cup cooked rice

1 avocado, halved, pitted, and peeled

½ pound sushi-grade yellowfin tuna, cut into ½-inch-thick slices

Sriracha Mayo, Wasabi Mayo, and Ginger Tamari Sauce (recipes follow), for drizzling

**1** In a small skillet, heat the oil over medium heat. When the oil is shimmering, add the French fries. Fry for about 5 minutes, using a slotted spoon or spider to turn occasionally, until crisp and browned. Transfer to a paper towel–lined plate and let cool completely.

**2** Arrange the nori sheets on a cutting board and divide the rice between them, leaving a ½-inch border. Arrange the avocado, tuna, and French fries on top of the rice and drizzle with the sauces. Roll the nori tightly around the filling (either like a sushi roll or burrito-style). Slice each roll in half and serve.

## VEGGIE ROLL

½ cup vegetable oil

1 (5-ounce) package sliced shiitake mushrooms

1 avocado, halved, pitted, peeled, and cut into ½-inch-thick slices

1 large egg, beaten

1 cup panko bread crumbs

Kosher salt

2 sheets nori

1 cup cooked rice

1 carrot, cut in thin matchsticks

1 cucumber, cut in thin matchsticks

Sriracha Mayo, Wasabi Mayo, and Ginger Tamari Sauce (recipes follow), for drizzling

**1** In a small skillet, heat the oil over medium heat. When the oil is shimmering, add the mushrooms and fry, stirring often, for about 5 minutes, until browned.

**2** While the mushrooms are cooking, combine the avocado and egg in a medium bowl and toss to coat. Transfer to a zip-top bag and add the panko. Seal the bag and toss to coat the avocado evenly, being careful not to break the slices.

*recipe continues*

**3** Transfer the mushrooms to paper towels and season with salt. Reserve the oil in the skillet, still over medium heat. Working in batches, add the avocado and fry for 3 to 4 minutes, flipping halfway through, until the panko crust is crisp and golden. Transfer to paper towels and season with salt. Repeat with the remaining avocado. Let the avocado cool slightly, until easy to handle, before assembling the rolls.

**4** Arrange the nori sheets on a cutting board and divide the rice between them, leaving a ½-inch border. Arrange the carrot, cucumber, avocado, and mushrooms over the rice and drizzle with the sauces. Roll the nori tightly around the filling (either like a sushi roll or burrito-style). Slice each roll in half and serve.

## SRIRACHA MAYO

**Makes ¼ cup**

¼ cup mayonnaise     1 tablespoon sriracha

Whisk the mayonnaise and sriracha in a small bowl. Transfer to a squeeze bottle or zip-top bag for easy drizzling.

## WASABI MAYO

**Makes ¼ cup**

¼ cup mayonnaise     1 teaspoon wasabi paste

Whisk the mayonnaise and wasabi in a small bowl. Transfer to a squeeze bottle or zip-top bag for easy drizzling.

## GINGER TAMARI SAUCE

**Makes ¼ cup**

¼ cup tamari     1 tablespoon minced fresh ginger

Whisk the tamari and minced ginger together in a small bowl.

# THANKSGIVING
## monte cristo

MAKES
1 SANDWICH

The age-old question: What to do with all those Thanksgiving leftovers? This! Green beans, sweet potato, cranberry sauce, turkey, and gravy all have a home here on this battered and fried (yep) sandwich. It makes a perfect next-day lunch or lazy dinner, or make it fresh for a visit to November anytime. (The gravy mayo is for making it on the fly; sub in real gravy if you're using leftovers.) It's turkey time!

½ cup cooked green beans

2 tablespoons dried cranberries

¼ cup sliced almonds

¼ cup store-bought crispy fried onions

¼ cup mayonnaise

2 teaspoons gravy powder

2 slices potato bread or your favorite sandwich bread

2 large eggs, lightly beaten

½ cup mashed cooked sweet potatoes

½ cup cranberry sauce, plus more for serving

4 slices turkey meat

1 tablespoon unsalted butter

**1** Slice the green beans on an angle in ½-inch-long pieces. Toss in a small bowl with the cranberries, almonds, and fried onions. Set aside.

**2** In a small bowl, whisk together the mayonnaise and gravy powder. Set aside. (You can skip this step if you're using leftover homemade gravy.)

**3** Dip one side of each slice of bread in the eggs, then place on a cutting board, dry-side up. Spread one slice with the sweet potatoes and the other slice with the cranberry sauce. Fold the turkey slices and pile them over the cranberry sauce. Spread the mayo mixture (or homemade gravy) over the turkey. Pile the green bean slaw on top of the sweet potatoes, then carefully place the turkey half of the sandwich on top.

**4** In a medium skillet, melt the butter over medium heat. Carefully place the sandwich in the skillet and fry on the first side for about 2 minutes, until golden brown, then flip and fry on the second side for about 2 minutes more, until golden brown.

**5** Slice the sandwich in half and serve with more cranberry sauce for dipping.

# BUFFALO CHICKEN
## *poutine* SERVES 2

### For the Fries

2 pounds russet potatoes, scrubbed and sliced into ½-inch pieces

1½ quarts vegetable oil

Kosher salt

### For the Poutine Topping

4 tablespoons (½ stick) unsalted butter

½ cup Buffalo hot sauce

½ pound ground chicken

1 large egg

1 teaspoon kosher salt

1 cup dried bread crumbs

1 tablespoon vegetable oil

Blue cheese crumbles, blue cheese dressing, thinly sliced celery, and thinly sliced scallions, for serving

Buffalo, New York, and Montreal, Quebec, aren't that far apart geographically, but couldn't be more different culturally. One is home to gorgeous architecture, cultural festivals, and Céline Dion. And the other is the home to the four-time Super Bowl—losing Buffalo Bills. Where they meet in the middle is incredible bar food: Buffalo's famous wings and Montreal's signature poutine. Why not combine the two for the best possible answer to afternoon beers with friends?

**1 Make the fries:** In a large pot, combine the potatoes and vegetable oil, ensuring the oil is covering the potatoes evenly. Set the pot over high heat and use a slotted spoon or spider to stir the fries. The oil will slowly warm up, then start to bubble. Continue to use the slotted spoon or spider to make sure no fries are stuck to the bottom or each other. The fries will slowly start to brown, then become crisp. When they're deep brown and very rigid, transfer the fries to a paper towel—lined plate and season well with salt. The entire process should take 20 to 30 minutes.

**2 Meanwhile, make the poutine topping:** In a large skillet, melt the butter over medium heat, then pour it into a medium bowl and set the skillet aside for later. Whisk the hot sauce into the melted butter.

**3** In a large bowl, combine the ground chicken, egg, salt, and half the hot sauce mixture. Use clean hands to break apart the chicken and evenly distribute the egg and hot sauce mixture. Add the bread crumbs and use clean hands to mix until combined (the mixture will be slightly sticky). Divide the chicken mixture into 10 meatballs and set aside on a plate.

*recipe continues*

**4** In the same skillet you used to melt the butter, heat the oil over medium heat. When the oil is shimmering, add the meatballs, leaving a little space between each one (do this in batches if necessary so as not to crowd the pan). Cook for about 5 minutes, until the bottoms are nicely browned, then flip the meatballs and add the remaining hot sauce mixture. Simmer for about 5 minutes, until the meatballs are cooked through. Remove from the heat.

**5** Arrange the fries on a large serving plate. Top with blue cheese crumbles, then arrange the meatballs on top. Pour the sauce remaining in the pan over the fries, then drizzle with blue cheese dressing. Top with celery and scallions and serve immediately.

# DORITOS & BEER
## baja tacos

SERVES 4 TO 6

What do Doritos, beer, and tacos have in common? (Besides all being in the stomach of a college kid on Saturday night.) Answer: They're all delicious! A bag of chips gets crushed into a delicious beer batter for these fish and shrimp tacos. After a quick fry, they're perfectly crisp and ready for warm corn tortillas and lots of fresh fixings. You know, to balance the beer and chips.

**1 Make the batter:** In a food processor or blender, pulse the chips for about 1 minute until broken down into fine crumbs. Transfer the crumbs to a large bowl, add the flour, cornstarch, baking powder, and adobo seasoning, and whisk to combine. Add the beer and whisk to combine. Set aside.

**2 Make the tacos:** In a large pot, heat the oil over medium-high heat until it reaches 350°F on an instant-read thermometer. Set a wire rack over a rimmed baking sheet and have it nearby.

**3** In a medium bowl, toss the cod and shrimp with the adobo seasoning. Set aside.

**4** In a medium bowl, toss the cabbage and vinegar with a generous pinch of salt and plenty of pepper. Set aside.

**5** When the oil reaches 350°F, working in batches, use tongs to coat the cod and shrimp in the beer batter and then gently lower them into the hot oil. Fry for about 4 minutes total, turning halfway, until deep orange and crisp. Use the tongs to transfer the fried cod and shrimp to the wire rack to cool. Repeat to batter and fry the remaining cod and shrimp.

*recipe continues*

### For the Beer Batter
1 (9.8-ounce) bag nacho cheese–flavored tortilla chips, such as Doritos

1 cup all-purpose flour

¼ cup cornstarch

1 tablespoon baking powder

1 tablespoon adobo seasoning

2 (12-ounce) cans lager beer

### For the Tacos
2 quarts (8 cups) vegetable oil

1 pound cod, cut in 1-inch strips

1 pound shrimp, peeled and deveined

1 tablespoon adobo seasoning

2 cups thinly sliced red cabbage

2 tablespoons cider vinegar

Kosher salt and freshly ground black pepper

12 6-inch corn tortillas, for serving

1 jalapeño, thinly sliced

1 (8-ounce) can crushed pineapple, drained

1 cup fresh cilantro leaves

**6** Set a gas burner to high or set a skillet over an electric burner on high. Heat the tortillas, one at a time, over the flame or in the skillet for 5 to 10 seconds per side, until soft and pliable. Transfer the tortillas to a clean dish towel as you go and cover to keep warm.

**7** Transfer the fried fish and shrimp to a serving plate. Serve with the cabbage slaw, jalapeño slices, pineapple, cilantro, and the warm tortillas on the side.

# tomato soup in a
# GRILLED CHEESE
# BREAD BOWL SERVES 2

1 boule or other round
bakery loaf

4 tablespoons (½ stick)
unsalted butter, at room
temperature

8 slices American cheese

1 (10.75-ounce) can tomato
soup

Spray cheese, fish-shaped
cheese crackers, chives, and
a pickle spear, for decorating
(optional)

All the comforts of childhood in a very adult portion, this bread
bowl gets the best fixings of a grilled cheese (plus an actual grilled
cheese made from the scraps!). The soup part is as easy as
popping open a can, because life should be simple. And adorable
decorations are optional but highly recommended for those who
still love to play with their food.

**1** Preheat the oven to 350°F and set a rack in the center. Line a
baking sheet with parchment paper.

**2** Use a knife to cut around the top of the bread, cutting down
but not all the way through the bottom and leaving about a
2-inch border. Use a spoon to scoop out the cut piece. (This will
become a grilled cheese, so pry it out carefully!)

**3** Set the bread bowl on the prepared baking sheet. Butter
the inside of the bread bowl with 3 tablespoons of the butter.
Arrange 6 slices of the cheese over the inside of the bread
bowl (they will stick to the butter). Bake for about 10 minutes,
until the cheese has melted.

**4** Meanwhile, heat a small skillet over medium-low heat.
Slice the reserved bread piece in half crosswise. Spread the
remaining 1 tablespoon butter over the cut side of each half.
Sandwich 2 slices of cheese between the bread. Fry the
sandwich for about 4 minutes on each side, until the bread is
nicely toasted and the cheese has melted.

**5** Remove the baking sheet from the oven, pour the tomato
soup into the bread bowl, and return the pan to the oven for
about 5 minutes more, until the soup is hot. Serve immediately,
with any desired decorations.

# GREEK SALAD
## in a salad bowl

### For the Chicken Skewers (optional)

1 pound boneless, skinless chicken thighs, cut into 1-inch cubes

2 tablespoons olive oil

2 tablespoons fresh lemon juice

1 tablespoon dried oregano

½ teaspoon kosher salt

½ teaspoon freshly ground black pepper

¼ teaspoon red pepper flakes

### For the Veggie Skewers (optional)

¼ cup ½-inch-thick half-moon zucchini slices

¼ cup ½-inch pieces yellow bell pepper

¼ cup cherry tomatoes

1 tablespoon olive oil

Why wash a bowl when you can just eat it? Iceberg lettuce is the perfect vessel for a fresh Greek salad, sturdy enough to hold the goods while also serving as a blank canvas for lots of flavor. This is a flexible recipe that can be made big enough for two or pulled back for one; sear the chicken skewers (for meat eaters) or the veggie skewers (for veggie eaters) or an optional both (for the over-the-top experience). And a toasted pita not only adds a base, it also soaks up all the delicious juices that seep through, offering you a perfect final bite to look forward to.

**1** **If making the chicken skewers:** In a zip-top bag, combine the chicken, oil, lemon juice, oregano, salt, black pepper, and red pepper flakes. Seal the bag tightly and toss to coat. Set aside to marinate at room temperature for 30 minutes.

**2** **If making the veggie skewers:** Use two of the skewers to skewer the zucchini, bell pepper, and tomatoes in an alternating pattern. Brush the veggies with the olive oil and set aside.

**3** **Make the salad:** Slice 2 inches off one side of the iceberg head and set aside. On the opposite side, slice off ¼ inch to create a flat surface so the head of lettuce stands upright. Stand the lettuce on a cutting board. Use a paring knife to cut out a circle from the top of the head, slicing all the way down, but not through, and leaving about a 1-inch border on all sides. Remove the lettuce core to create your bowl. On the cutting board, thinly slice the core and sliced-off pieces of lettuce into long strips.

**4** Combine the sliced lettuce, cucumber, tomatoes, and olives in a medium bowl. Add the oil, lemon juice, oregano, salt, and pepper and toss to combine. And the feta and gently fold to combine. Set aside.

**5** Heat a large skillet over medium heat. Skewer the chicken (if using) onto the two remaining skewers. Add the skewers to the skillet and cook until the chicken is lightly charred on all sides and cooked through, about 5 minutes total. Transfer the chicken skewers to a plate. Add the veggie skewers (if using) to the skillet and cook, rotating to cook on all sides, for about 5 minutes, until the veggies are charred. Transfer to the plate with the chicken skewers.

**6** Warm the pita in the skillet for about 1 minute per side, then transfer to a plate. Place the iceberg bowl on top of the pita. Fill the bowl with the dressed salad. Lay the chicken and veggie skewers over the top and serve immediately.

*For the Salad*

1 medium head iceberg lettuce

¼ cup half-moon cucumber slices

¼ cup cherry tomatoes, halved

¼ cup pitted olives (preferably Kalamata)

1 tablespoon olive oil

1 tablespoon fresh lemon juice

1 teaspoon dried oregano

¼ teaspoon kosher salt

¼ teaspoon freshly ground black pepper

2 ounces feta cheese, crumbled (about ½ cup)

1 or 2 pitas

*Special Equipment*

4 wooden skewers (or 2 skewers, if only making the veggie skewers), trimmed to fit into your skillet

# samosa
# BAKED POTATO SALAD

Baked potatoes are warm and comforting, but need a lot of seasoning to cross into the realm of delicious. Instead of the usual pile of sour cream, chives, cheese, and bacon, try a vegetarian version that's heavy on the spices with a refreshing herb chutney to balance it out. It's like three delicious potato dishes in one: all the crispy skin of a twice-baked potato, a savory interior piled high like a potato salad, plus fried wonton strips to mimic the flaky pastry of a samosa.

**1 Make the potato salad:** Preheat the oven to 400°F and set a rack in the center.

**2** Set the potato on a sheet of foil and prick it all over with a fork. Rub the skin with 1 tablespoon of the oil and season generously with salt. Wrap the potato tightly in the foil and bake, directly on the oven rack, for about 30 minutes, until a knife easily slides into the potato.

**3** Meanwhile, in a small skillet, heat the remaining ½ cup oil over medium heat. Carefully drop the wonton strips into the oil and fry, using a slotted spoon to turn them once, for about 1 minute, until curled and golden brown all over. Use the slotted spoon to transfer the wonton strips to a paper towel to drain.

**4** Pour 1 tablespoon of the frying oil into a medium bowl. Add the turmeric, cumin, coriander, cardamom, ginger, chili powder, salt, and pepper. Stir until the mixture is well combined and resembles a paste. Add the peas and mayonnaise and stir to combine.

*recipe continues*

**SERVESV 1**

**For the Potato Salad**

1 large russet potato

½ cup plus 1 tablespoon vegetable oil

½ teaspoon kosher salt

1 square wonton wrapper, sliced into ½-inch-wide strips

½ teaspoon ground turmeric

½ teaspoon ground cumin

½ teaspoon ground coriander

½ teaspoon ground cardamom

½ teaspoon ground ginger

½ teaspoon chili powder

½ teaspoon kosher salt

½ teaspoon freshly ground black pepper

¼ cup frozen peas

2 tablespoons mayonnaise

**For the Chutney**

6 fresh mint leaves

2 sprigs of cilantro

1 (1-inch) piece fresh ginger, peeled

1 garlic clove, peeled

1 jalapeño, halved and seeded

2 tablespoons vegetable oil

**5** Remove the potato from the oven and transfer to a cutting board (keep the oven on). Discard the foil and allow the potato to cool. When the potato is cool enough to handle, slice off the top third (on the long side) to create a boat shape, reserving the sliced-off portion. Scoop out almost all the potato flesh, leaving a ½-inch border all around the inside. Coarsely chop the slice of potato and the scooped-out flesh into small cubes, then add them to the spiced mayonnaise mixture and toss to coat. Fill the potato boat with the spiced potato mixture and set it on a rimmed baking sheet. Bake for about 10 minutes, until the skin is crisp and the filling is warmed through.

**6** **Meanwhile, make the chutney:** In a blender, combine the mint, cilantro, ginger, garlic, jalapeño, oil, and 2 tablespoons water. Blend on high for about 1 minute, until the mixture is smooth, scraping down the sides as needed. Transfer to a bowl and set aside.

**7** Transfer the loaded potato to a plate and drizzle with the chutney as desired. (Refrigerate any remaining chutney in an airtight container for up to 5 days.) Top with the fried wontons and serve immediately.

# cowboy caviar
# MINESTRONE SOUP

Cowboy caviar, or Texas caviar, is a dip of black-eyed peas and chopped veggies in a zippy vinaigrette. Minestrone is a warm pot of soup made with beans, chopped veggies, and pasta in broth. With more in common than not, it only seemed obvious that the two should meet and form an alliance. All the deep comfort of a steaming bowl of soup, all the fresh flavors of tangy dip, all the going back for comforting seconds.

**1** In a Dutch oven or other large pot, heat the oil over medium heat. When the oil is shimmering, add the bell pepper, onion, and jalapeño. Cook, stirring occasionally, for about 5 minutes, until the onion and pepper have begun to soften. Add the cumin, chili powder, oregano, salt, and black pepper. Stir and cook for about 1 minute, until the spices are fragrant.

**2** Add the salsa, black beans, black-eyed peas, corn, and broth and increase the heat to high. Bring the mixture to a boil, then add the pasta and cook, stirring occasionally, for about 8 minutes, or until al dente according to package directions.

**3** Remove the minestrone from the heat and add the cilantro, scallions, and vinegar. Divide among bowls and top with tortilla chips. Serve immediately.

## SERVES 8

2 tablespoons olive oil

1 green bell pepper, stemmed, cored, and coarsely chopped

1 red onion, coarsely chopped

1 jalapeño, seeded and diced

2 tablespoons ground cumin

1 tablespoon chili powder

1 tablespoon dried oregano

2 teaspoons kosher salt

½ teaspoon freshly ground black pepper

1 (15.5-ounce) jar chunky salsa

1 (15.5-ounce) can black beans, drained and rinsed

1 (15.5-ounce) can black-eyed peas, drained and rinsed

1 (15.25-ounce) can corn, drained

1 (32-ounce) container vegetable broth

1 cup dried elbow-shaped pasta

½ cup finely chopped fresh cilantro

4 scallions, thinly sliced

3 tablespoons red wine vinegar

Crushed tortilla chips, for serving

# SLOPPY JOE

## *double bacon cheeseburger*

SERVES 4

8 slices thick-cut bacon, halved crosswise (optional), or 2 tablespoons vegetable oil

1 pound ground beef or ground meat substitute

1 cup ketchup

2 dill pickle spears, diced, plus 2 tablespoons brine from the pickle jar

2 tablespoons (packed) light brown sugar

1 tablespoon Worcestershire sauce

1 tablespoon Dijon mustard

2 teaspoons smoked paprika

1 teaspoon chili powder

½ teaspoon kosher salt

8 slices American cheese

1 red bell pepper, stemmed, cored, and diced

½ white onion, diced

4 sesame buns, halved

The only thing that could make a double bacon cheeseburger more exciting is bringing in the Joe—sloppy Joe. The patty mix gets hit with ketchup, a ton of seasonings, bacon, cheese, and—twist!—pickle brine. Then it's shaped into burgers, pan-seared, and topped with more bacon, cheese, and pickles for a seriously delicious, sloppy burger that barely hangs on to the bun.

**1** In a 12-inch cast-iron skillet or a large nonstick skillet, cook the bacon (if using) over medium heat, flipping occasionally, for about 10 minutes, until the bacon is crisp and the fat has rendered. Transfer the bacon to paper towels and remove the skillet from the heat (reserve the bacon fat for later).

**2** In a large bowl, combine the ground beef, ketchup, pickle brine, brown sugar, Worcestershire, mustard, paprika, chili powder, and salt. Use clean hands to break apart the beef and combine the ingredients until the mixture is homogenous.

**3** Set 8 of the bacon pieces on a cutting board and cut into ¼-inch pieces. Add them to the beef mixture and stir to combine. Stack 4 slices of American cheese together and cut the stack into 3 strips, then cut the strips crosswise to make 12 squares. Add the cheese to the beef mixture, then add the bell pepper. Use clean hands to combine until everything is evenly incorporated. Form the beef mixture into 4 equal patties.

**4** In a medium bowl, toss the diced dill pickle with the onion to combine. Set aside.

**5** Return the skillet with the bacon fat to the stove and heat over medium heat (or heat the vegetable oil in a clean skillet if omitting the bacon). When the fat is shimmering, add the burger patties to the skillet, leaving plenty of room between each (cook them in batches if necessary). Cook for about 5 minutes, until the bottoms are nicely browned, then flip the burgers and top evenly with the remaining slices of cheese and pieces of bacon. Cook for about 5 minutes more, until the burger is cooked through and the cheese has melted.

**6** Arrange the buns on a serving platter or on separate plates and transfer each burger to the bottom half of each bun. Spoon the pickle-onion mixture on top of the burgers before topping with the bun tops. Serve immediately.

# BRUSSELS SPROUT & MUSHROOM "BACON" carbonara

**SERVES 4**

### For the Parm Crisps
½ cup grated Parmesan

2 teaspoons smoked paprika

### For the Mushroom "Bacon"
½ cup sliced shiitake mushrooms

1 teaspoon smoked paprika

1 teaspoon (packed) light brown sugar

1 teaspoon Worcestershire sauce

1 teaspoon tamari

¼ teaspoon kosher salt

¼ teaspoon freshly ground black pepper

1 tablespoon vegetable oil

### For the Carbonara
1 tablespoon plus ½ teaspoon kosher salt

4 large egg yolks

1 large egg

¼ cup grated Parmesan

¼ teaspoon freshly ground black pepper

1 tablespoon vegetable oil

½ pound Brussels sprouts, trimmed and halved

16 ounces dried linguine

Brussels sprouts and bacon are a classic pair, this we know. But a smoky, savory, super simple mushroom "bacon" is an over-the-top meatless swap for a vegetarian dish that feels totally indulgent. Once the veggies are beautifully browned, a creamy carbonara sauce blankets the dish, plus a beautiful Parmesan crisp rests on top of the pasta pile to help send your lunchtime over the top.

**1** Preheat the oven to 400°F and set a rack in the center. Line a rimmed baking sheet with a silicone baking mat or parchment paper.

**2** **Make the Parm crisps:** Form the grated Parmesan into 3-inch rounds on the prepared baking sheet, using 2 tablespoons for each and leaving plenty of room between them. Bake for 3 to 5 minutes, until the cheese has melted into a light golden brown crisp. Let cool for 5 minutes.

**3** Use two small pieces of a paper towel to cover each Parm crisp, leaving a diagonal stripe exposed down the center. Sprinkle ½ teaspoon of the paprika over the exposed portion of each crisp. Set aside.

**4** **Make the mushroom "bacon":** In a small bowl, toss the mushrooms with the paprika, brown sugar, Worcestershire, tamari, salt, and pepper until well combined and coated.

**5** In a large skillet, heat 1 tablespoon of the oil over medium heat. When the oil is shimmering, add the mushrooms in a single layer, leaving space between each one. Fry, stirring occasionally, for about 6 minutes, until the mushrooms are crisp. Transfer to a small bowl and set aside. Wipe out the skillet.

**6** **Make the carbonara:** Fill a large pot with water and add 1 tablespoon of the salt. Bring to a boil over high heat.

**7** Meanwhile, in a medium bowl, whisk together the egg yolks, egg, Parmesan, pepper, and the remaining ½ teaspoon salt. Set aside.

**8** In the same large skillet from the mushrooms, heat 1 tablespoon of the oil over medium heat. When the oil is shimmering, add the Brussels sprouts to the skillet in an even layer. Season with a generous pinch of salt and a few grinds of pepper. Cook, tossing occasionally, for about 10 minutes, until the sprouts are browned in spots and tender when pricked with a fork.

**9** While the Brussels sprouts cook, add the linguine to the boiling water and cook until al dente according to the package directions. Use a measuring cup to scoop out 2 cups of the pasta water, then drain the linguine and return it to the pot.

**10** Slowly whisk ½ cup of the reserved pasta water into the bowl with the egg mixture, then gently pour the mixture over the pasta and use tongs to toss. Toss continuously while adding the Brussels sprouts, bacon, and ½ cup more pasta water, until the linguine is glossy and evenly coated and the sauce has thickened. Taste for seasoning, adding more salt and pepper as needed.

**11** Divide the pasta among four plates, lifting and twirling it into small mounds. Perch a Parm crisp on top of each serving and serve immediately.

# GRILLED BLT *salad*

With all the deliciousness of a BLT but a very heavy tilt toward the L, this healthy-ish salad-for-lunch is anything but boring. Crisp bacon is coated in a sticky glaze, slices of bread are slathered in mayo and grilled for crunchy croutons, the tomatoes and romaine get an extra-delicious char on the grill, and the whole shebang is finished with a tangy, creamy dressing. Hey, we said healthy-*ish*.

**1** Heat a grill to medium-high or heat a grill pan over medium-high heat.

**2** **Make the dressing:** In a medium bowl, whisk together the mayonnaise, mustard, vinegar, sugar, salt, and black pepper. Set aside.

**3** **Make the salad:** In a medium bowl, use clean hands to toss the bacon with the brown sugar, maple syrup, and cayenne. Fold a piece of bacon into a ribbon pattern and slide it halfway down 1 wooden skewer. Fold another piece of bacon and slide it onto the same skewer. Repeat with the remaining bacon and the second skewer.

**4** Brush the grill grates or pan with 1 tablespoon of the oil. Grill the bacon skewers, turning to cook on all sides, for about 4 minutes, until crisp and golden. Transfer to a plate.

**5** Spread the mayonnaise on both sides of the bread slices. Grill the bread for about 2 minutes per side, until toasted and crisp. Transfer to a cutting board and cut into 1-inch cubes.

**6** Carefully place the cherry tomatoes on the grill, with the vine facing up, and grill for about 3 minutes, until the tomatoes are charred and blistered. Transfer to the plate with the bacon.

**7** Brush the romaine halves with the remaining 2 tablespoons oil. Grill, cut-side down, for about 5 minutes, until charred.

**8** Transfer the romaine to a serving platter. Spoon about half the dressing over the romaine. Top with the bread cubes and arrange the bacon and tomatoes alongside. Spoon over the remaining dressing and serve immediately.

**SERVES 2**

*For the Dressing*
½ cup mayonnaise

2 tablespoons Dijon mustard

2 tablespoons white wine vinegar

1 teaspoon sugar

½ teaspoon kosher salt

½ teaspoon freshly ground black pepper

*For the Salad*
4 slices thick-cut bacon

2 tablespoons (packed) light brown sugar

2 tablespoons pure maple syrup

Pinch of cayenne pepper

3 tablespoons vegetable oil

2 tablespoons mayonnaise

2 slices white bread

8 ounces cherry tomatoes on the vine

2 romaine hearts, halved lengthwise

*Special Equipment*
2 wooden skewers, soaked in a large bowl of water for 10 minutes

# ATOMIC BROWN SUGAR
## beer can chicken

1 (16-ounce) can lager beer

2 tablespoons (packed) light brown sugar

1 tablespoon kosher salt

1 teaspoon freshly ground black pepper

1 teaspoon smoked paprika

1 teaspoon chili powder

1 teaspoon cayenne pepper

½ teaspoon red pepper flakes

½ teaspoon dried oregano

½ teaspoon mustard powder

½ teaspoon onion powder

½ teaspoon garlic powder

1 (3- to 4-pound) chicken, rinsed and patted dry with paper towels

2 tablespoons unsalted butter, melted

The grill-season classic comes inside for an easy oven-roast chicken with all the juicy interior and crisp exterior you know and love. While the beer can adds insane moisture from the breast to the drum, it's not the most extreme element of this baby. It's actually the spice rub, made with smoky paprika, brown sugar, oregano, and cayenne (it's right on the edge of too spicy but so good), that pushes this bird over the top. It's best carved into pieces and drizzled with the incredibly savory pan sauce, but if you just tear into it with your hands and drag it through the pools of sauce in the pan, no judgment.

**1** Preheat the oven to 450°F and set a rack in the center. Crack open the beer can, then use a can opener to remove the entire top. Set the can in the center of an 8-inch square baking pan.

**2** In a medium bowl, stir together the brown sugar, salt, black pepper, paprika, chili powder, cayenne, red pepper flakes, oregano, mustard powder, onion powder, and garlic powder. Pour 1 tablespoon of the spice mixture into the beer can (the beer will bubble over into the pan).

**3** Rub the skin of the chicken all over with the melted butter. Sprinkle 2 tablespoons of the spice mixture into the cavity of the chicken, then rub the remaining spice mixture all over the outside of the bird, rubbing some under the breast skin and coating the legs and wings thoroughly.

**4** Set the chicken cavity on top of the beer can until the legs barely touch the baking dish—the can should hold the chicken upright. Carefully set the pan in the oven and bake the chicken for 30 to 40 minutes, until the thickest part of the thigh reaches 165°F on an instant-read thermometer.

*recipe continues*

**5** Remove the pan from the oven and let the chicken rest on the can for about 15 minutes, then use tongs to carefully remove the chicken (take care, as the can—and the beer in the can—may still be hot) and transfer it to a cutting board. Discard the beer and the can. Carve the chicken (see below) and arrange the pieces on a serving platter. Drizzle the pan juices over the chicken and serve immediately.

TIP: To move this recipe onto the grill, set one side of the grill to high heat (450°F) and keep the other side cool. Follow the recipe exactly, except set the pan holding the chicken on the cool side and cook over indirect heat for about 1 hour, until the thigh meat reaches 165°F.

## How to Carve a Chicken

**1** Place the chicken on a sturdy cutting board. Grab a big fork and a sharp knife.

**2** Starting on one side, slide your knife between the drumstick and the breast, using your fork to pull the drumstick away. Continue to cut down through the thigh until you hit the hip joint. Press hard to cut through the joint while pulling the thigh away with the fork.

**3** Cut through the connective joint between the thigh and drumstick. Transfer these pieces to a serving tray.

**4** Use the fork to find the spine in the center of the breast. Slide your knife just next to the spine until you hit the ribs. Use your fork to peel back the breast, and continue to run your knife just next to the ribs until you hit the wing joint. Press hard to cut through the joint while pulling the breast away with the fork.

**5** Cut through the connective joint between the wing and breast. Transfer these pieces to the serving tray.

**6** Repeat on the other side.

**7** Over-the-top move: Freeze the carcass to make stock later.

# OKONOMIYAKI *ramen*

Okonomiyaki is a savory Japanese pancake; its name is a combination of the words *okonomi* ("what you like") and *yaki* ("cooked"). In that spirit, there are endless regional variations throughout the country, with endless preferences for fillings and preparations. But the common thread in all great okonomiyaki is a ton of green cabbage and an umami-rich sauce that is basically Japan's answer to Worcestershire sauce. (We'll teach you how to make an easy substitute below.) Ramen, another Japanese staple, has similarly endless possibilities for delicious toppings. So why not have the best of both worlds: a steaming-hot bowl of ramen, topped with cabbage, sauces, tempura, and the classic soft-boiled egg. Warm, filling, nourishing, and very over the top.

**1 Make the sauce:** In a small bowl, whisk together the ketchup, Worcestershire, sugar, and tamari. Set aside.

**2 Make the ramen:** Fill a medium saucepan with water and bring to a boil over high heat. Carefully lower the egg into the water and boil for 7 minutes. Drain the egg and run under cold water until cool enough to handle. Set aside.

**3** Cook the ramen according to the package directions, including the seasoning packet. Pour the finished ramen into a large serving bowl. Pile the cabbage on top and add tempura chips as desired. Peel the egg, slice it in half, and place it on top of the ramen. Drizzle the okonomiyaki sauce over the top in a zigzag and drizzle mayonnaise in an opposite zigzag. Finish with scallions and serve immediately.

## SERVES 1

*For the Okonomiyaki Sauce*

¼ cup ketchup

3 tablespoons Worcestershire sauce

2 tablespoons sugar

2 tablespoons tamari

*For the Ramen*

1 large egg

1 (3-ounce) package dried ramen noodles (with seasoning packet)

1 cup shredded green cabbage

Tempura chips, mayonnaise, and thinly sliced scallions, for serving

# BBQ *sheet pan supper*

The success of this recipe hinges on one thing: how tightly you can seal foil. Otherwise, it's pretty much just tossing together a spice rub, mixing a few ingredients for the sides, placing everything on a sheet pan, opening the oven door, and sliding it in. Brisket and ribs get coated in a dry rub, wrapped, and baked. Then foil packets of collards, mac, and beans all join the party for the last half. When everything is done, it's as easy as unwrapping, slicing, and diving in. The fragrance wafting off the tray is pure OMGBBQ!

**1** Preheat to 350°F and set a rack in the center. Line a rimmed baking sheet with foil.

**2** **Make the spice rub:** In a medium bowl, whisk together the brown sugar, paprika, salt, garlic powder, onion powder, black pepper, cayenne, cumin, and oregano. Scoop 2 tablespoons of the spice mixture into a small bowl. Set both bowls aside.

**3** **Make the BBQ:** Lay two long sheets of foil on top of each other. Place the brisket in the center, with the fat facing up. Pour about half the spice rub from the larger bowl onto the brisket and rub it all over the sides to coat the brisket thoroughly. Fold the foil up and around the brisket, creating an open basket, making sure the sides are completely sealed. Pour in 2 cups water then tightly seal the top. Place the brisket on the prepared baking sheet.

**4** Lay two more long sheets of foil on top of each other. Place the ribs in the center. Pour the remaining spice rub from the larger bowl over the ribs and rub it all over to coat the ribs thoroughly. Wrap the ribs tightly in the foil and transfer to the baking sheet.

*recipe continues*

### For the Spice Rub
¼ cup light brown sugar

¼ cup smoked paprika

3 tablespoons kosher salt

2 tablespoons garlic powder

2 tablespoons onion powder

1 tablespoon black pepper

2 teaspoons cayenne pepper

2 teaspoons ground cumin

1 teaspoon dried oregano

### For the BBQ
2 pounds brisket

1 rack baby back ribs (about 1½ pounds), cut in half

½ cup barbecue sauce

### For the Sides
1 bunch collard greens, leaves stemmed and chopped

6 garlic cloves, smashed

½ stick beef jerky, halved and cut into ½-inch pieces

1 (15.5-ounce) can navy beans, drained and rinsed

¼ cup ketchup

½ cup barbecue sauce

1 cup elbow-shaped pasta

2 slices American cheese

2 cups shredded cheddar

1 cup whole milk

Crushed baked cheese crackers, coleslaw, pickle slices, and sliced white bread

**5** Bake the brisket and the ribs for 1 hour 30 minutes.

**6 Meanwhile, make the sides:** Cut six 8-inch square sheets of foil. Stack two sheets on top of each other and fold up the sides to create a bowl shape; repeat with the remaining sheets of foil to make two more bowls.

**7** Place the collards, garlic, and beef jerky in one foil bowl, then season with salt and black pepper. Pour in 1 cup water, then seal the top of the bowl tightly. In the second foil bowl, combine the navy beans, ketchup, barbecue sauce, and reserved 2 tablespoons spice rub and stir to combine, then seal the top of the bowl tightly. In the third foil bowl, combine the pasta, American cheese, and cheddar cheese, along with some salt and black pepper to taste. Pour in the milk, then seal the top of the bowl tightly.

**8** Remove the baking sheet from the oven. Add the three foil packets to the baking sheet, stacking them on top of the meat. Return the baking sheet to the oven and cook for 1 hour 30 minutes more.

**9** Transfer the foil packets to a work surface and carefully open the tops to release the steam. Stir the pasta and top with crushed crackers. Stir the baked beans and collards. Fold down the sides of all the packets so they resemble serving bowls.

**10** Transfer the ribs to a cutting board and discard the foil. Slather the racks with the barbecue sauce, then cut them into individual ribs. Return them to the baking sheet.

**11** Transfer the brisket to the cutting board. Carefully roll back the foil (there will still be liquid inside), pour out the liquid, and discard the foil. Slice the brisket into 1-inch-thick pieces, then return it to the baking sheet. Set the foil bowls on the baking sheet alongside the brisket and ribs. Arrange piles of coleslaw, pickles, and bread on the pan alongside the meat and sides, then serve.

# PIZZA on PIZZA

What's the one thing pizza has always lacked? More pizza, duh! A skillet pizza suddenly becomes a party with not one, not two, but THREE layers of pizza piled on top. The standard crust, sauce, cheese, and pepperoni form the base, then pizza snack rolls make up the crust, while pizza bagels fill in the center. Over the top? Yes. Delicious? Chyeah.

1 ball store-bought pizza dough (about 8 ounces), at room temperature

2 tablespoons vegetable oil

1 cup store-bought pizza sauce

1½ cups shredded Italian-blend cheese

12 pepperoni slices

1 (7.5-ounce) box frozen pizza snack rolls

1 (7-ounce) box frozen pizza bagels

**1** Preheat the oven to 500°F and set a rack in the center. Place a 12-inch cast-iron skillet on the center rack to preheat.

**2** Stretch the pizza dough into a round about 12 inches in diameter. Remove the skillet from the oven and add the oil, swirling the skillet to coat the bottom. Carefully place the pizza dough in the skillet, stretching it more if necessary to fill the surface area. Spoon the pizza sauce over the dough, leaving a 1-inch border. Sprinkle the cheese over the entire pizza round, including over the border. Arrange the pepperoni around the pizza, leaving a 1-inch border. Place the pizza snack rolls in an overlapping layer around the border, turning them to the long side to fit on the crust. Place 4 pizza bagels on the pizza.

**3** Reduce the oven temperature to 350°F and bake the pizza for about 15 minutes, until the cheese has melted and the crust is golden brown and crisp. Remove from the oven and let cool in the skillet for about 5 minutes to let the cheese set. Slide the pizza onto a cutting board and slice into four pieces, then serve.

# SPICY MAPLE CHICKEN & WAFFLE *sandwich*

## For the Marinade

2 cups whole milk

Juice of 1 lemon

1 teaspoon kosher salt

1 teaspoon black pepper

½ teaspoon cayenne pepper

4 boneless, skinless chicken thighs (about 1 pound)

## For the Maple Candy

1 cup sugar

½ cup pure maple syrup

1 tablespoon baking soda

Flaky sea salt and cayenne

## For the Fried Chicken

2 cups all-purpose flour

1 tablespoon garlic powder

1 tablespoon dried oregano

1 tablespoon kosher salt

2 teaspoons black pepper

1½ teaspoons cayenne

8 cups vegetable oil

## For the Sandwich

8 frozen waffles, thawed

4 tablespoons (½ stick) unsalted butter

3 tablespoons maple syrup

¼ teaspoon cayenne pepper

What makes this sandwich extraordinary? It's not the tender-marinated chicken that gets double-dredged for an extra-crispy-crunchy coated fried chicken. It's not the slathering of gooey maple butter dripping down the fried chicken and pooling in the divots of the tender golden waffles. No, it's the sweet, spicy, salty, and crunchy maple candy sprinkled over the top (get it?) that really sends this into orbit. (Btw, toss that leftover maple candy in an airtight container and do your best not to snack on it throughout the week.)

**1 Make the marinade:** In a large bowl, whisk together the milk, lemon juice, salt, black pepper, and cayenne. Add the chicken thighs and cover the bowl tightly with plastic wrap. Marinate in the refrigerator for at least 1 hour or up to 24 hours.

**2 Meanwhile, make the candy:** Line a rimmed baking sheet with a silicone baking mat or parchment paper. Combine the sugar, maple syrup, and ¼ cup water in a medium saucepan and clip a candy thermometer to the side. Bring to a boil over high heat—do not stir; the sugar will dissolve in the liquid. As soon as the mixture reaches 300°F, remove it from the heat and quickly whisk in the baking soda. When the mixture bubbles and rises, use a spatula to scrape it onto the prepared baking sheet. Immediately sprinkle the mixture with flaky salt and cayenne. Let cool completely, about 1 hour, then break the candy into bite-size pieces. (The candy can be stored in an airtight container at room temperature for up to 1 week.)

*recipe continues*

**3 Fry the chicken:** In a medium bowl, whisk together the flour, garlic powder, oregano, salt, black pepper, and cayenne.

**4** In a Dutch oven or other large pot, heat the oil over medium-high heat until it reaches 350°F on an instant-read thermometer.

**5** When the oil is at temperature, use tongs to transfer each chicken thigh from the marinade to the flour mixture. Toss to coat thoroughly. Transfer the chicken back to the marinade, then toss in the flour again (this is the double-dredge). Add all 4 chicken thighs to the hot oil and cook for about 8 minutes total, turning the thighs after 4 minutes, until the chicken is crisp and golden brown. (An instant-read thermometer inserted into each thigh should read 165°F.) Transfer the chicken to a paper towel–lined plate or a wire rack set over a rimmed baking sheet.

**6** **Make the sandwich:** Toast the waffles and arrange them in pairs on serving plates.

**7** Combine the butter and maple syrup in a small microwave-safe bowl. Microwave on high for about 30 seconds, until the butter is melted. Stir in the cayenne and set aside.

**8** Divide the fried chicken among the plates, placing each thigh on top of one waffle. Drizzle with the maple butter. Set the other waffle on top to make a sandwich and drizzle with more maple butter. Sprinkle the maple candy on top of each sandwich and secure the waffles with decorative skewers. Serve immediately.

# PHILADELPHIA
## *poke tots bowl*

Tater tots are incredible, no arguments there. But tots made from fried sushi rice instead of potatoes? Truly over the top! All the incredible flavors of America's favorite roll are rearranged in this poke bowl, like smoked salmon, cucumber, and avocado, plus a wasabi cream cheese sauce and a sprinkle of seaweed and sesame seeds finish off a stunning presentation that's almost too beautiful to eat.

**1 Make the tots:** Cook the rice according to the package directions. In a large bowl, whisk together the vinegar, sugar, and salt, then add the cooked rice and toss to coat. Set aside to cool completely, about 1 hour. (The tots are easiest to make with cooled rice.)

**2 Meanwhile, make the sauce:** In a small bowl, whisk together the cream cheese, milk, wasabi, and ginger. Set aside.

**3 Fry the tots and assemble the bowls:** When the rice is cool, in a Dutch oven or other large pot, heat the oil over medium-high heat until it reaches 375°F on an instant-read thermometer.

**4** Use wet hands to form the rice into 1-inch cylinders about the size of tater tots. Working in batches, add the rice tots to the oil, about 12 at a time, being careful not to crowd them, and fry, turning occasionally, for about 3 minutes, until golden brown. Transfer the rice tots to a paper towel–lined plate and sprinkle with salt. Repeat to fry the remaining tots.

**5** Divide the tots between two bowls. Drape half the lox over each bowl of tots, then top each bowl evenly with the avocado, cucumber, and seaweed. Drizzle tamari over each bowl, then top each with a scoop of the cream cheese sauce. Sprinkle with sesame seeds and serve immediately.

*For the Tots*

2 cups sushi rice

3 tablespoons rice vinegar

2 tablespoons sugar

1 teaspoon kosher salt, plus more as needed

*For the Cream Cheese Sauce*

2 ounces cream cheese

2 tablespoons whole milk

½ teaspoon wasabi

½ teaspoon ground ginger

*To Assemble*

2 quarts (8 cups) vegetable oil

4 ounces lox

½ avocado, halved, pitted, peeled, and cubed

½ cucumber, cut into matchsticks

2 seaweed snacks, cut in thin strips

Tamari and sesame seeds, for serving

# fried egg RAVIOLI

**SERVES 2**

1 tablespoon kosher salt, plus more as needed

24 circular wonton wrappers

½ cup ricotta cheese

12 medium egg yolks

Flaky sea salt, freshly ground black pepper, and hot sauce, for serving

At last, a ravioli that's as visually hilarious as it is delicious! To make these ravs, which look like perfectly fried sunny-side-up eggs, just add ricotta to a round wonton wrapper, nestle in an egg yolk, seal with a second wonton wrapper, then boil! Cutting into a perfectly oozing yolk makes this dish feel equally rich and exciting. We love a simple splash of hot sauce to finish them off, but marinara or a cream sauce would of course be the right answer, too.

**1** Bring a large pot of water to boil over high heat. Add the salt.

**2** Place 12 wonton wrappers on a work surface. Scoop four ½-teaspoon mounds of ricotta onto each wrapper, leaving a ½-inch border and the wrapper exposed in the center of the ricotta scoops. Add an egg yolk to the center of each ricotta circle. (It should look like a fried egg with very puffy whites.) Season the ricotta and yolk with a pinch of salt on each wrapper.

**3** Fill a small bowl with cold water. Working one at a time, dip a finger into the bowl and wet the edges of one of the filled wrappers. Place one of the remaining unfilled wrappers on top and press firmly to seal the edges, being careful not to break the yolk. Repeat with the remaining wrappers.

**4** When the water is boiling, use a spider skimmer or a slotted spoon to gently lower 6 of the ravioli into the pot. Boil, undisturbed, for 3 to 5 minutes, until the ravioli are al dente and translucent. Transfer the ravioli to a paper towel–lined plate and repeat with the remaining 6 ravioli.

**5** Arrange the ravioli on a serving plate or individual plates. Season with flaky salt and plenty of pepper. Finish with a drizzle of hot sauce and serve.

# salad PARTY PLATTER

**For the Cucumber Vinaigrette**

½ cucumber, peeled, halved lengthwise, and seeded

2 tablespoons olive oil

Zest and juice of 1 lime

2 tablespoons chopped fresh chives

2 tablespoons fresh parsley leaves

1 teaspoon Dijon mustard

1 teaspoon kosher salt

**For the Blackberry Dressing**

8 ounces fresh blackberries

¼ cup plain Greek yogurt

¼ cup olive oil

¼ cup white wine vinegar

1 tablespoon honey

1 teaspoon kosher salt

2 tablespoons chopped fresh basil leaves

For a dinner party kickoff that is truly over the top, start with this salad platter. (Think of it as the love child of a cheese plate and the salad course.) Make the dressings up to 2 days ahead and refrigerate until it's go time. For the salad itself, scale up or down depending on the size of the group. Then arrange everything over a table or a large board, winding a path of leaves across the space and nestling groups of toppings in each curve along the way. Let each person make their way down the line to build a dream salad right on their plate!

**1 Make the vinaigrette:** In a blender, combine the cucumber, oil, lime zest and juice, chives, parsley, mustard, and salt. Blend on high for about 1 minute, until smooth. Pour into a serving bowl and set aside. Rinse out the blender jar.

**2 Make the blackberry dressing:** In the blender, combine the blackberries, yogurt, oil, vinegar, honey, and salt. Blend on high for about 1 minute, until smooth. Pour into a serving bowl and stir in the basil. Set aside.

**3 Create the platter:** Arrange the salad greens over a large serving surface in an overlapping, winding pattern. Arrange the bowls of dressing and salad accompaniments along the curves, then serve, allowing everyone to create their own salads.

*For serving*

Radicchio leaves

Butter lettuce leaves

Blue cheese

Gouda cheese

Marinated artichoke hearts

Pitted olives

Pickled red onions

Seedless grapes

Sliced apples

Thinly sliced celery

Tamari almonds

Cheese twists

# WHOLE ROASTED FISH
## with sizzling chili crisp

SERVES 4

Pouring sizzling-hot oil over anything takes it over the top, but over a gorgeous whole fish? Forget about it. Make it sizzling-hot chili crisp, and bang!—total mic drop. (Chili crisp, a Chinese condiment that is basically the best thing ever, is a perfect mix of crunchy bits of garlic and shallot, spicy chili, and salty-savory notes, all bathed in oil.) The good news is, roasting a whole fish is easy and super forgiving. The meat will stay moist even if it's in the oven a little too long. The better news is, we also broke it down to a single serving if you feel like pulling out all the self-care stops for yourself (see page 96). And that can easily be doubled to two servings when it's time to impress your special fish in the sea.

**1** **Make the fish:** Preheat the oven to 450°F and set a rack in the center. Line a rimmed baking sheet with parchment paper.

**2** Place the fish on the prepared baking sheet. Open the cavity of the fish and season both sides of the flesh with a big pinch of salt. Arrange the garlic cloves near the spine. Lay the fish flat and arrange the slices of orange, lemon, and lime in the cavity.

**3** Roast the fish for about 30 minutes, until an instant-read thermometer inserted into the flesh near the head reads 135°F.

**4** **Meanwhile, make the chili crisp:** In a small saucepan, combine the shallot, garlic, cinnamon, anise, cardamom, peppercorns, and oil. Heat over low heat, stirring occasionally, for about 20 minutes, until the shallot and garlic are crisp and browned (they will slowly fry as the oil heats up). Set a fine-mesh strainer over a medium bowl and strain the oil into the bowl; pour the oil back into the saucepan and set over high heat. Discard the cinnamon stick and anise pods and transfer the rest of the spices to the same medium bowl. Add the peanuts, Aleppo pepper, red pepper flakes, white sesame seeds, black sesame seeds, sugar, salt, and nori and stir to combine. Pour the oil into the medium bowl over the spices. (Careful, it will sizzle!) Set aside.

**5** Transfer the fish to a serving platter and top with mint and cilantro leaves. Spoon the chili crisp around the fish on the serving platter. Serve immediately.

*For the Fish*
1 (3- to 4-pound) whole red snapper, scaled and cleaned

Kosher salt

4 garlic cloves, smashed and peeled

1 orange, sliced into ½-inch-thick rounds and seeded

1 lemon, sliced into ½-inch-thick rounds and seeded

1 lime, sliced into ½-inch-thick rounds and seeded

*For the Chili Crisp*
1 small shallot, halved and thinly sliced

6 garlic cloves, thinly sliced

3 whole cinnamon sticks

2 star anise pods

3 whole cardamom pods, smashed

1 tablespoon whole black peppercorns

2 cups peanut oil

¼ cup peanuts, chopped

2 tablespoons Aleppo pepper

1 tablespoon red pepper flakes

1 tablespoon white sesame seeds

1 tablespoon black sesame seeds

1 tablespoon sugar

1 tablespoon kosher salt

1 sheet nori, thinly sliced

Torn fresh mint and cilantro leaves, for serving

*recipe continues*

# SINGLE-SERVING ROASTED FISH

1 (4- to 6-ounce) frozen fish fillet, such as cod or tilapia

1 teaspoon olive oil

Kosher salt and freshly ground black pepper

½ lemon, sliced into ½-inch-thick rounds and seeded

Chili Crisp (see page 95)

Torn fresh mint and cilantro leaves

**1** Preheat the oven to 450°F and set a rack in the center. Line a rimmed baking sheet with parchment paper.

**2** Run the frozen fillet under cold water to remove any ice crystals. Pat dry and brush on both sides with the oil. Season with a generous pinch of salt and a few cracks of black pepper on both sides. Place the fillet on the prepared baking sheet and top with the lemon slices.

**3** Transfer the fish to the oven and roast for 8 to 12 minutes, until an instant-read thermometer inserted into the thickest part reads 135°F. (Meanwhile, prepare the chili crisp as directed.)

**4** Transfer the fish to a plate and top with mint and cilantro leaves. Spoon a small portion of the chili crisp around the fish, then let the extra chili crisp cool and transfer it to an airtight container. Store in the refrigerator for up to 1 month.

## How to Serve a Whole Fish

**1** Use a knife to gently slice where the fillet meets the head, then make another slice where the fillet meets the tail.

**2** Starting at the head, cut along the backbone toward the tail. Slide the knife under the fillet and use a fork to help lift it away from the spine. Set the fillet on a plate, skin-side down.

**3** Lift the tail, then slide the fork underneath to help pry the spine away as you continue to lift the bones. The head should come along with everything else. Discard the bones and head.

**4** Run your hand over both fillets to check for any remaining bones to pull out. Slide your knife under the first fillet and use a fork to help transfer it back on top of the second fillet, skin-side up.

# LASAGNA FLORENTINE
## *galette*

SERVES 4

A galette is a rustic tart made by folding a pie dough crust over sweet or savory ingredients. But you know what's easier than making and rolling out pie dough? Boiling noodles! This pasta galette is almost like a lasagna—except all the filling goes in the center and the noodles fold up and around the fillings, rather than being layered with them. Slathered in Alfredo sauce and Parmesan, the noodle crust epitomizes everything you love about lasagna corners and edges, with a satisfyingly cheesy spinach-fortified filling that sticks to the ribs.

**1** Preheat the oven to 375°F and set a rack in the center. Line a rimmed baking sheet with parchment paper.

**2 Make the filling:** In a medium bowl, stir together the spinach, ricotta, Alfredo sauce, garlic, salt, black pepper, and red pepper flakes. Set aside.

**3 Make the galette:** Bring a large pot of salted water to a boil. Add the lasagna noodles and cook according to package directions. Drain and let cool slightly.

**4** Transfer the lasagna noodles to a cutting board and cut each in half crosswise. Arrange 4 lasagna pieces in a cross shape on the prepared baking sheet. Place 4 additional pieces in the spaces between the first 4 pieces to form a second cross shape, slightly overlapping the first. Repeat with the remaining 8 pieces to create a full circle.

**5** Spoon the filling into the center of the lasagna noodle circle and use a spatula to spread the mixture into an even layer, leaving a 3-inch border. Dollop 2 tablespoons of the ricotta over one area of the filling. Dollop the remaining ricotta into

*For the Filling*
1 (10-ounce) package frozen spinach, thawed and drained
¼ cup ricotta cheese
¼ cup store-bought Alfredo sauce
2 garlic cloves, thinly sliced
½ teaspoon kosher salt
¼ teaspoon freshly ground black pepper
¼ teaspoon red pepper flakes

*For the Galette*
8 dried lasagna noodles
½ cup ricotta cheese
¼ cup store-bought Alfredo sauce
Grated zest of ½ lemon
Freshly ground black pepper
Parmesan cheese

*recipe continues*

four mounds of 2 tablespoons each across the surface of the filling.

**6** Brush the exposed border of the lasagna noodles with some of the Alfredo sauce. Fold the border over the filling and brush the tops with more Alfredo. Brush the entire lasagna noodle "crust" with the remaining Alfredo.

**7** Sprinkle the lemon zest over the exposed filling, then top with a good amount of black pepper. Grate Parmesan generously over the lasagna noodle "crust."

**8** Bake for 20 to 25 minutes, until the "crust" is golden brown. Let the galette cool on the baking sheet for about 15 minutes to set before slicing and serving.

# maple pecan potato swirl
# SHEPHERD'S PIE

SERVES 8

### For the Pie

2 tablespoons olive oil

3 medium carrots, diced

3 stalks celery, diced

1 small shallot, diced

3 garlic cloves, minced

Kosher salt and freshly ground black pepper

1 (6-ounce) can tomato paste

1 (32-ounce) container vegetable broth

1 cup dried brown lentils

### For the Topping

Kosher salt

½ pound sweet potato, peeled and cut into cubes

2 cups whole milk

2 pounds russet potatoes, peeled and cut into cubes

½ cup raw unsalted pecans

1 tablespoon (packed) light brown sugar

1 tablespoon pure maple syrup

This hearty vegetarian dish will hit the spot for all appetites. And with a visually stunning presentation, it's not too hard on the eyes, either. A very savory veggie and lentil stew fills in the bottom, while orange sweet potato twirls and swirls with white mashed potatoes on top. Rows of pecans (or a pecan spiral, if you're feeling artsy) accent the top for a very over-the-top finish.

**1** **Make the pie:** In a 12-inch cast-iron skillet, heat the oil over medium heat. When the oil is shimmering, add the carrots, celery, shallot, and garlic; season with salt and pepper. Cook, stirring occasionally, for about 10 minutes, until the carrots are crisp-tender and the celery and shallot are translucent.

**2** Stir in the tomato paste and broth and increase the heat to high. Bring the mixture to a boil, then add the lentils. Boil for about 10 minutes, until the lentils are tender. Turn off the heat and let the mixture cool.

**3** **Make the topping:** Preheat the oven to 350°F and set a rack in the center.

**4** Fill a large pot with water and plenty of salt. Bring to a boil over high heat. Add the sweet potato and cook for about 10 minutes, until a knife easily slides through a piece. Use a slotted spoon or strainer to transfer the sweet potato to a medium bowl, reserving the boiling water. Add ½ cup of the milk and a generous pinch of salt to the sweet potato, then mash with a potato masher; set aside.

**5** Add the russet potatoes to the boiling water and cook for about 10 minutes, until a knife easily slides through a piece. Drain the potatoes and transfer them to a large bowl. Add the remaining 1½ cups milk and a generous pinch of salt, then mash with a potato masher.

**6** Spoon the russet potatoes on top of the lentil mixture in the skillet and use the back of the spoon to smooth into an even layer. Dot the sweet potatoes across the top in random places. Use a fork to drag across the potatoes diagonally in one direction, then diagonally in the other direction, to create a crosshatch pattern while distributing the sweet potato.

**7** In a small bowl, toss the pecans with the brown sugar, maple syrup, and a pinch of salt to coat. Line up the pecans in diagonal rows over the potatoes. Transfer the skillet to the oven and bake for 15 to 20 minutes, until the potatoes and pecans are browned and the pie is heated through to the center. Serve immediately.

# PASTRY-WRAPPED HOLIDAY HAM
## *with cider glaze*

Who knows how pineapple and maraschinos became synonymous with ham, but they are arguably the original over-the-top garnish. A dish that screams "old-fashioned" in the best way possible, this little ham gets wrapped in store-bought crescent roll dough (you know the one!) that bakes into a crisp golden brown crust. The sliced ham gets a spoonful of tangy apple cider sauce for a perfect accent. But we all know the real stars are those yellow and red circles covering the surface. Don't settle for regular toothpicks here; find some real showstoppers to rise to the occasion.

**1 Make the ham:** Preheat the oven to 350°F and set a rack in the center. Line a baking sheet with parchment paper.

**2** In a small bowl, whisk together the brown sugar and mustard until combined.

**3** Score the top of the ham diagonally in one direction, making cuts about 1 inch apart and about ¼ inch deep, then score diagonally in the opposite direction. Brush the mustard mixture all over the ham. Set the ham on the prepared baking sheet and bake for about 20 minutes, until the ham is golden on the outside and an instant-read thermometer inserted into the thickest part of the meat registers 160°F.

**4** Spread out the crescent dough as one intact sheet on a work surface. Remove the baking sheet from the oven (keep the oven on) and use tongs to transfer the ham to the center of the dough. Wrap the dough around the ham to cover it, then brush with the egg. Return the ham to the oven and bake for about 20 minutes more, until the pastry crust is golden brown and flaky.

**5 Meanwhile, make the cider glaze:** In a medium saucepan, combine the apple cider, vinegar, honey, mustard, and chili powder and bring to a boil over medium-high heat. Reduce the heat to medium-low and simmer for about 10 minutes more, until the sauce is slightly reduced and thickened.

**6** Transfer the ham to a serving platter. Set a pineapple ring on the surface of the ham, then hold a maraschino cherry in the center. Stick a toothpick through the cherry to hold it in place. Repeat to cover the ham with pineapple and cherries. Pour the cider glaze into a gravy boat to pass at the table.

**SERVES 4**

*For the Ham*
¼ cup (packed) light brown sugar

¼ cup Dijon mustard

1 (1½- to 2-pound) smoked boneless ham

1 (8-ounce) tube crescent roll dough

1 egg, beaten

*For the Cider Glaze*
1 cup apple cider

⅓ cup cider vinegar

⅓ cup honey

1 tablespoon Dijon mustard

1 teaspoon chili powder

Pineapple rings and maraschino cherries, for serving

# sweet DREAMS

# FUNNEL CAKE
## *banana split*

A banana split already goes above and beyond with literally most every sundae topping showing up to the party. Adding a whole funnel cake as the base of your split creates a sundae experience you never knew you needed. An easy batter made from pancake mix gets drizzled into oil in a hot pan for a quick shallow fry. From there, it's up to your imagination. Pile on the ice cream into a sky-high tower or stay low and let the whipped cream do the work. There's no wrong answer, and approximately one gazillion right ones.

**1** In a medium bowl, whisk together the pancake mix, sugar, vanilla, and ¼ cup water until combined. Pour the mixture into a small zip-top bag.

**2** In a small skillet, heat the oil over medium heat. Dip the handle of a wooden spoon in the oil; if the oil bubbles rapidly, it's ready.

**3** Snip the tip off the zip-top bag and carefully but quickly squeeze all the batter into the skillet in a circular pattern. Fry the dough for about 2 minutes, until the bottom is golden, then use tongs to flip and fry for about 2 minutes more, until the second side is golden. Use the tongs to transfer the funnel cake to a wire rack set over paper towels. Let cool.

**4** Place the funnel cake on a serving plate and scoop some ice cream on top. Cut a banana in half lengthwise and arrange the halves on either side of the ice cream. Scoop more ice cream on top, then drizzle with hot fudge, caramel, and strawberry sauce as desired. Top everything with sprinkles. Dollop with whipped cream and finish with a cherry. Serve immediately, with two spoons.

½ cup store-bought pancake mix

1 tablespoon sugar

1 teaspoon vanilla extract

1½ cups vegetable oil

*For serving*

Ice cream

Banana slices

Hot fudge

Caramel

Strawberry sauce

Sprinkles

Whipped cream

Maraschino cherries

# lemon meringue BARS

**MAKES 12 BARS**

## For the Crust
Nonstick cooking spray

1 (14.4-ounce) box graham crackers

¾ cup (packed) light brown sugar

1 cup (2 sticks) unsalted butter, melted

## For the Lemon Filling
2 (3-ounce) boxes lemon gelatin mix

1 cup boiling water

1 (8-ounce) container whipped topping

## For the Meringue
¾ cup egg whites (about 6 large), at room temperature

½ cup granulated sugar

½ teaspoon cream of tartar

Here you get all the delicious elements of a classic lemon meringue pie in a weirdly adorable bar form. A graham cracker crust and lemon filling come together in a flash and can chill in the fridge for up to 24 hours for an easy make-ahead dessert. Then it's creativity time! A simple meringue is the ideal vessel for the swirls and shapes of your dreams. A quick toast in the oven sets the meringue pieces and gives them a perfect golden hue. Place them all over the finished bars for a wild journey down Lemon Meringue Lane.

**1** **Make the crust:** Line a 9 by 13-inch baking dish with plastic wrap. Cut a 9 by 17-inch piece of parchment paper and layer it on top of the plastic wrap, leaving a 2-inch overhang on two sides. Coat the parchment and plastic wrap with nonstick spray.

**2** Unwrap all the graham crackers and put them in a food processor, breaking up the sheets by hand as you go. Add the brown sugar and process for about 2 minutes, scraping down the sides as needed, until the mixture consists of fine crumbs. Add the melted butter and process for about 30 seconds more, until the mixture resembles wet sand.

**3** Pour the graham cracker mixture into the prepared baking dish and gently press it into an even layer over the bottom. Set the crust aside.

**4** **Make the lemon filling:** Empty the packets of lemon gelatin mix into a medium bowl. Pour in the boiling water and whisk to fully dissolve the gelatin. Whisk in the whipped topping until incorporated. Pour the lemon filling over the graham cracker crust. Cover loosely with plastic wrap and refrigerate for at least 2 hours to set the filling or up to 24 hours if making ahead.

*recipe continues*

**5 Make the meringue:** Preheat the oven to 375°F and set two racks in the upper and lower thirds. Line two rimmed baking sheets with silicone baking mats or parchment paper and coat the mats or parchment with nonstick spray.

**6** In a large bowl using an electric mixer, beat the egg whites on low speed until frothy. Gradually increase the speed to high and beat until the egg whites hold soft peaks. Add the granulated sugar and cream of tartar and beat until the meringue holds stiff peaks. Transfer the meringue to a piping bag fitted with a wide tip (or see page 35; if you want the meringue to have ridges, be sure to use a star tip).

**7** Pipe the meringue onto the prepared baking sheets in circles of various sizes from ½ inch to 2 inches. Bake for 10 minutes, rotating the pans and swapping their positions in the oven halfway through, until the meringues are golden brown in places and slightly dehydrated. Let cool on the baking sheets for 10 minutes.

**8** Remove the baking dish from the refrigerator. Run a knife around the edge of the pan. Carefully lift the bars from the dish using the overhanging parchment and transfer the whole thing to a cutting board. Use an offset spatula to lift the meringues from the baking sheet and arrange them over the lemon filling. Cut into 12 bars, then serve from the cutting board.

# *giant* LAVA CAKE   SERVES 8

If you've ever wondered what to get a lava cake lover for their birthday—oh, here's an idea—make them a Giant Lava Cake. This is extravagant, this is indulgent, this is definitely over the top. It's also insanely simple. Chocolate cake mix in a Bundt pan, check. Dark chocolate melted in cream, check. Cocoa powder and decorations on top, check. This easy dessert is perfect for celebrations or a big finish to any dinner.

Nonstick cooking spray

1 box chocolate cake mix, plus any ingredients specified on the box

16 ounces dark chocolate, chopped

2 cups heavy cream

Unsweetened cocoa powder, for dusting

Sparklers, candles, and decorative picks, for serving

**1** Preheat the oven to 350°F and set a rack in the center. Lightly coat a Bundt pan with nonstick spray.

**2** Prepare the cake batter according to the package directions, then pour it into the prepared Bundt pan. Bake for 35 to 45 minutes, until a toothpick inserted into the center comes out clean. Set aside to cool in the pan.

**3** Put the chocolate in a medium bowl. In a small saucepan, heat the cream over medium-high heat just until it comes to a boil, 3 to 5 minutes. Pour the hot cream over the chocolate and whisk until the chocolate has melted and the mixture is smooth.

**4** Invert the cooled Bundt cake onto a large serving plate, preferably with a rim (large enough to handle and catch a lot of lava flow) and gently tap to release the cake. Pour the melted chocolate mixture into the center of the cake and let it spill over the sides. Dust the cake all over with cocoa powder. Decorate with any finishing touches, like sparklers, candles, or decorative picks, before slicing.

# THREE-LAYER
## *magic cake*

Nonstick cooking spray

4 large eggs, separated, at room temperature

1 cup sugar

½ cup (1 stick) unsalted butter, melted

¾ cup all-purpose flour

2 cups whole milk

1 packet unsweetened drink mix, such as Kool-Aid, in any color

2 cups heavy cream

¼ cup store-bought blueberry jam

Sprinkles, for topping

What starts as a very runny batter somehow transforms into three distinct layers. It has something to do with the oven and the space-time continuum, big-brain stuff. But what comes out is pure magic: The bottom layer is almost a gelatin, the middle layer is a jiggly custard, and the top layer is soft cake. It can be made plain for a simple white cake, but this book isn't called *Plain*. So grab that packet of fruity drink mix (like Kool-Aid) and make a vibrant, tangy, and somehow not-too-sweet cake that will make a real impact.

**1** Preheat the oven to 325°F and set a rack in the center. Line an 8-inch square baking dish with an 8 by 12-inch piece of parchment paper, leaving a 2-inch overhang on two sides. Coat the parchment and exposed pan sides with nonstick spray.

**2** In a large bowl using an electric mixer, beat the egg yolks and sugar until pale and fluffy, starting on low speed and slowly increasing to high to avoid splatter. Add the melted butter and flour and beat until no flour streaks remain. Add the milk and the drink mix and beat until completely incorporated.

**3** Clean the beaters very well with hot, soapy water (even a trace of fat will prevent the egg whites from forming stiff peaks). In a medium bowl using the electric mixer, beat the egg whites until they hold stiff peaks. Using a spatula, gently fold about one-fourth of the egg whites into the batter, being careful not to deflate them. Repeat to fold in the remaining egg whites, leaving some patches of unincorporated whites. The batter will be very runny.

**4** Pour the batter into the prepared pan. Bake for 50 to 60 minutes, until a toothpick inserted into the center comes out clean and the cake is just slightly wobbly. Let the cake cool completely in the pan, about 1 hour. Use the overhanging parchment to lift the cake out of the pan and transfer it to a serving dish or platter. Use scissors to trim the sides of the parchment flush with the sides of the cake.

**5** **Make the frosting:** In a medium bowl using an electric mixer, beat the cream until it holds stiff peaks, starting on low speed and slowly increasing to high. Add the jam and whip again to stiff peaks. Spread the frosting over the top of the cake in an even layer and use an offset spatula or butter knife to swoop it into peaks. Top the cake with sprinkles, then slice into 9 squares. Serve immediately.

# CANDY BAR
## *ice cream sandwiches*

MAKES
8 ICE CREAM
SANDWICHES

Brownies, ice cream, candy bars. Why choose?! For those who can never have enough chocolate, we present an almost inappropriate amount of chocolate. Boxed-mix brownies (kind of the best brownies?) get loaded with chopped-up candy bars, then are used to sandwich candy bar ice cream, then are covered in chocolate shell, sprinkles, glitter, and whatever your heart desires. It's a frozen treat that's almost too cool to eat.

**Nonstick cooking spray**

**1 box fudgy brownie mix, plus any ingredients specified on the box**

**8 mini chocolate candy bars, halved and thinly sliced**

**1 (1.5-quart) container chocolate candy bar ice cream**

**1 (7.25-ounce) container chocolate coating, such as Magic Shell**

**Sprinkles, edible glitter, or candy, for topping**

**1** Preheat the oven to 350°F and set a rack in the center. Coat an 8-inch square baking dish with nonstick spray.

**2** Prepare the brownie batter according to the package directions. Fold in the chopped candy bars. Pour the batter into the prepared baking dish and bake for about 40 minutes (the brownies will bake longer than the package specifies because of the added candy bars), until a toothpick inserted into the center comes out clean (test it in a few spots, because the candy pieces will still be fudgy even if the brownies are cooked through). Let the brownies cool completely in the baking dish. Remove the brownies, wrap tightly in plastic wrap, and freeze for 1 hour.

**3** Line an 8-inch square baking dish with an 8 by 10-inch piece of parchment paper, leaving a 1-inch overhang on two sides. Remove the ice cream from the freezer and allow it to soften, about 5 minutes. Slice the brownies in half horizontally to create two 8-inch square pieces. Place the bottom slice in the prepared baking dish. Scoop the ice cream in several scoops over the brownie slice in the baking dish, then use a spatula to spread the ice cream into an even layer. Set the other brownie slice on top to create a large ice cream sandwich. Cover the dish in plastic wrap and return to the freezer to chill for 1 hour.

**4** Use the overhanging parchment to lift the ice cream sandwich from the baking dish and set it on a cutting board. Slice it in half lengthwise, then crosswise, to create four even squares. Cut each square in half to create 8 rectangular ice cream sandwiches total. Space the sandwiches evenly across the baking sheet. Working one at a time, drizzle the chocolate coating over the sandwiches, letting it run down the sides. Quickly sprinkle any toppings over the sandwiches while the coating is still wet. Freeze once more until ready to serve.

# PARTY *krispies*

Nonstick cooking spray

4 tablespoons (½ stick) unsalted butter

1 (10-ounce) bag mini marshmallows

6 cups crisp rice cereal

White chocolate chips, peanut butter chips, sprinkles, fruity crisp rice cereal, crushed chocolate sandwich cookies, and pretzels, for topping

Rice Krispies Treats are a gold-standard dessert. So how to take the classic treat over the top? Sprinkle lots of things, well, over the top. Chocolate chips, rainbow sprinkles, cereal, cookies, and pretzels are all invited to this party. Scale up or scale back as needed; just aim for lots of color, texture, and flavor for over-the-top snap, crackle, and pop.

**1** Coat a 9 by 13-inch baking dish with nonstick spray.

**2** In a large Dutch oven, heat the butter over low heat until just melted (don't let it start to foam; otherwise, the marshmallows could scorch as they melt). Add the marshmallows and cook, stirring frequently, until completely melted. Remove from the heat and add the cereal. Fold to coat the cereal in the marshmallow mixture.

**3** Coat a silicone spatula with nonstick spray. Use the spatula to scoop the cereal mixture into the prepared baking dish and press it into an even layer. Cover the surface with white chocolate chips, peanut butter chips, sprinkles, fruity crisp rice cereal, crushed chocolate sandwich cookies, and pretzels (the majority will stick to the cereal mixture just fine). Transfer the dish to the refrigerator to chill for 30 minutes before cutting into 9 pieces. Serve immediately.

# mexican hot chocolate
# PUSH-UP POPS

**MAKES 20 ICE CREAM POPS**

4 cups heavy cream, very cold

1 cup unsweetened cocoa powder

2 teaspoons vanilla extract

2 teaspoons ground cinnamon

2 teaspoons chili powder

½ teaspoon kosher salt

¼ teaspoon cayenne pepper

2 (14-ounce) cans sweetened condensed milk

*Special Equipment*
20 push-up pop molds

Mexican baking chocolate is made with spices like ground cinnamon, vanilla bean, chili powder (made from ground chiles, not the spice blend), and cayenne to make chocolaty cocoa powder much more complex and interesting. An easy whipped cream base with sweetened condensed milk turns the spiced cocoa into a rich and creamy ice cream pop dessert. Molds for push-up pops are easy to find online; if you prefer a traditional scoop, freeze the base in a 9 by 5-inch loaf pan to make ice cream, or divide it into popsicle molds for a fudgy, melty treat.

**1** Set a sturdy cardboard box on a rimmed baking sheet and poke 20 holes in the box, spacing them 2 inches apart. Remove the caps from the push-up pop molds and retract the base of each mold to its full length. Stand the molds upright by sliding the sticks through the holes in the cardboard box. Set aside.

**2** In a large bowl using an electric mixer, beat the cream, cocoa powder, vanilla, cinnamon, chili powder, salt, and cayenne on low speed until combined. Gradually increase the speed to high to whip the cream mixture to soft peaks. Pour in the condensed milk and beat briefly on low speed to incorporate.

**3** Spoon the mixture into the molds, using a skewer or chopstick to release any air bubbles. Freeze for at least 4 hours before serving. (The pops will keep for up to 2 weeks.)

# BLUEBERRY CORNMEAL

#  bars MAKES 12 BARS

Okay, we know what you're thinking. Blueberry and corn? Weird! Well, stop thinking that, because blueberry and corn? Delicious! Corn's laid-back sweetness pairs so well with blueberry's tart personality for a match made in heaven. A delicious cornmeal crust gets piled with plump blueberries. Then more cornmeal gets crumbled on top. And then, because we're so extra, fresh corn and cornflakes get sprinkled over the final dish for a bar that hits so many layers of flavor, texture, and sweetness.

**1** Preheat the oven to 350°F and set a rack in the center. Coat a 9 by 13-inch baking dish with nonstick spray.

**2 Make the blueberry filling:** In a medium bowl, combine the blueberries, lemon zest and juice, brown sugar, cornstarch, and salt. Use clean hands to toss the mixture, being careful not to crush the berries. Set aside.

**3 Make the cornmeal crust:** In a large bowl, whisk together the egg, brown sugar, baking powder, cinnamon, and salt until combined. Add the cornmeal, flour, and butter and use clean hands to squeeze the mixture into a soft, crumbly dough.

**4** Evenly sprinkle about half the crust mixture (about 2 cups) over the bottom of the prepared baking dish, pressing it into a thin, even layer. Pour the blueberry filling over the top, then crumble the remaining crust mixture in various-sized pieces over the filling. Bake for 35 to 40 minutes, rotating the baking dish halfway through, until the crumble topping has begun to brown.

**5** Remove the baking dish from the oven and top with the corn kernels and cornflakes. Let cool in the pan for about 30 minutes before slicing into 12 bars.

Nonstick cooking spray

*For the Blueberry Filling*
4 cups fresh blueberries
Zest and juice of 1 lemon
½ cup (packed) light brown sugar
1 tablespoon cornstarch
½ teaspoon kosher salt

*For the Cornmeal Crust*
1 large egg
½ cup (packed) light brown sugar
1 teaspoon baking powder
1 teaspoon ground cinnamon
½ teaspoon kosher salt
1½ cups cornmeal
1½ cups all-purpose flour
1 cup (2 sticks) unsalted butter, at room temperature
1 cup thawed frozen or drained canned corn kernels
1 cup frosted cornflakes

# CARAMEL APPLE
## cone-noli  [MAKES 8 CONES]

If you love cannoli, look no further—you've found your anytime-craving hack with these ricotta cream–filled sugar cones. A layer of warm and buttery sautéed caramel apples brings the whole situation to new heights, while a drizzle of more caramel (always more caramel!) and a dusting of powdered sugar finish the effect. It's totally over the top with middle-of-the-road effort.

½ cup ricotta cheese

1 cup powdered sugar, plus more for dusting

1 (8-ounce) package cream cheese, at room temperature

2 tablespoons unsalted butter

2 Granny Smith apples, peeled, cored, and diced

¼ cup (packed) light brown sugar

1 teaspoon ground cinnamon

½ teaspoon kosher salt

8 sugar cones

Store-bought caramel sauce and butterscotch chips, for serving

**1** In a medium bowl, whisk together the ricotta and powdered sugar until combined. Add the cream cheese and whisk again until smooth. Transfer the ricotta filling to a piping bag fitted with a wide tip (or see page 35), set the bag upright in a large glass, and refrigerate for 30 minutes.

**2** Meanwhile, in a medium skillet, melt the butter over medium heat. Add the apples and stir to coat in the butter. Cook the apples for about 5 minutes, until they have softened slightly. Add the brown sugar, cinnamon, and salt and cook, stirring occasionally, for about 5 minutes more, until the apples are coated in a thick, gooey mixture. Remove from the heat and set aside.

**3** Dip the rim of a sugar cone in caramel sauce, then pipe about 1 tablespoon of the ricotta filling into the bottom of the cone. Add 2 tablespoons of the apple mixture, then pipe about ¼ cup of the filling on top. Sprinkle butterscotch chips over the top and set the cone on a serving plate. Repeat with the remaining cones and filling. Dust the finished cones with more powdered sugar and serve.

# strawberry SHORTICECREAMCAKE

**SERVES 6**

2 cups heavy cream

1 (14-ounce) can sweetened condensed milk

1 teaspoon vanilla extract

1 tablespoon finely chopped fresh mint

1 cup store-bought strawberry preserves or jam

1 (10.75-ounce) frozen pound cake, thawed

1 (8-ounce) container whipped topping

1 tablespoon ground freeze-dried strawberries, for serving

Strawberry shortcake, the ideal of early summer flavors, is a treat worth waiting (all year) for. Ice cream cake is the ideal of a low-effort, no-bake, make-ahead dessert. Mash the two together . . . Do you see where this is going? You guessed it! All the flavors of both, turbocharged into a refreshing dessert that's just . . . ideal! Bonus: Using strawberry jam means that this dessert can be made any time your life needs a little summer breeze.

**1** Line a 9 by 5-inch loaf pan with plastic wrap, leaving about 3 inches of overhang on each side.

**2** In a large bowl using an electric mixer, whip the cream until stiff peaks form, starting on low speed and slowly increasing to high. Pour in the condensed milk and vanilla and whip to stiff peaks. Transfer 2 cups of the cream mixture to a medium bowl and fold in the mint. Set aside. Fold the strawberry preserves into the remaining cream mixture in the large bowl.

**3** Spread about half the strawberry cream into the prepared loaf pan. Slice the pound cake horizontally into a ½-inch-thick piece, mimicking the shape of the loaf pan. Place the slice of pound cake in the pan on top of the strawberry cream and use the remaining strawberry cream to fill in the sides (reserve the remaining pound cake for another use). Spread the mint cream on top of the loaf and strawberry cream and smooth the top. Loosely cover the baking dish with the overhanging plastic wrap and freeze for at least 6 hours or up to 24 hours.

**4** Unwrap the cake and invert it onto a serving plate; discard the plastic. Spread the whipped topping evenly over the top and sides of the cake, then use an offset spatula or butter knife to create swoops. Dust the top with the freeze-dried strawberries. Slice and serve immediately.

# BANANA PUDDING
## cream puffs

Cream puffs are already so ridiculous, they're almost over the top on their own. But when you add a delicious banana pudding (from a box, relax!) and then delicious touches like banana slices, marshmallow, and vanilla wafers . . . well, these puffs ascend to a whole other level. (See page 126 for step-by-step photos.)

**1 Make the puffs:** Preheat the oven to 400°F and set a rack in the center. Line a rimmed baking sheet with a silicone baking mat or parchment paper.

**2** In a medium saucepan, combine the butter, brown sugar, salt, and ½ cup water and bring to a boil over medium-high heat. As soon as the butter has fully melted and the mixture is boiling, add the flour and use a wooden spoon to stir until the dough comes together to form a ball. Cook, stirring occasionally, for about 5 minutes more, until the dough is fragrant and glossy.

**3** Remove the saucepan from the heat and let cool for 5 minutes (it is important for the mixture to cool enough that when you add the eggs, they won't begin to cook).

**4** Add the vanilla and 1 egg and stir to incorporate; the mixture will seem wet and broken, but will pull together into a stiff dough. Add the second egg and stir to incorporate. Transfer the dough to a piping bag fitted with a star tip (or see page 35).

**5** Lightly whisk the egg white in a small bowl. Pour a little water into a separate small bowl. Pipe the dough onto the prepared baking sheet into 14 even rounds, about 1½ inches in diameter and 2 inches apart. Dip a finger in the bowl of water and lightly tap the peak of each round to smooth the top, then

### For the Puffs
2 tablespoons unsalted butter

1 tablespoon (packed) light brown sugar

¼ teaspoon kosher salt

½ cup all-purpose flour

½ teaspoon vanilla extract

2 large eggs

1 large egg white

### For the Banana Pudding
1 (3.4-ounce) box banana pudding mix

1¼ cups whole milk

1 banana, sliced into 28 (¼-inch-thick) rounds

Marshmallow creme and crushed vanilla wafers, for serving

*recipe continues*

lightly brush the rounds with the egg white. Bake for about 25 minutes, until puffed and golden brown. Let cool completely on the baking sheet, about 1 hour.

**6** **Make the pudding:** In a medium bowl, whisk together the pudding mix and milk until very thick. (It will be thicker than a normal pudding, to make it easier to fill the puffs.) Transfer the pudding to a piping bag fitted with a star tip (or see page 35).

**7** Slice the cooled puffs in half horizontally. Set a banana round in the base of each puff. Dip the tops of the puffs in the marshmallow creme and sprinkle with some crushed vanilla wafers. Pipe the pudding onto the banana slice and set the top half of the puff over the pudding. Set a banana slice on top and use a toothpick to secure it to the puff. Serve immediately.

# COCONUT
## ice cream cake

Calling all coconut lovers—have we got a cake for you! First we boost a boxed cake mix with toasted coconut flakes. Then we make the easiest ice cream from condensed milk, coconut candy bars, and cream. Finally, the entire cake gets covered in coconut frosting and pink (!) coconut flakes. We're nutty for coco!

**1 Make the cake:** Preheat the oven to 350°F and set a rack in the center. Coat a 10-inch springform pan with nonstick spray.

**2** Spread half the coconut flakes in an even layer over a rimmed baking sheet (reserve the remaining coconut flakes for the frosting). Toast in the oven for 5 to 7 minutes, stirring halfway through, until the coconut is lightly golden brown. Transfer the toasted coconut to a medium bowl.

**3** Add the cake mix to the bowl with the toasted coconut and prepare the batter according to the package directions. Pour the batter into the prepared springform pan. Bake the cake for about 40 minutes, until a toothpick inserted into the center comes out clean. Let cool in the pan for 30 minutes, then remove the springform ring and lift the cake from the pan base onto a wire rack to finish cooling. Reassemble the springform pan and spray it with nonstick spray.

**4 Make the ice cream layer:** In a large bowl using an electric mixer, beat the cream until it holds stiff peaks, starting on low speed and slowly increasing to high. Pour in the condensed milk and whip to stiff peaks once more. Add the chopped candy bars and briefly beat on low speed to incorporate. Pour the mixture into the prepared springform pan. Cover the surface loosely with plastic wrap and freeze for 1 hour.

*recipe continues*

### For the Cake
Nonstick cooking spray

1 (14-ounce) bag sweetened coconut flakes

1 box white cake mix, plus any ingredients specified on the box

### For the Ice Cream Layer
2 cups heavy cream

1 (11-ounce) can condensed coconut milk

1 (11.3-ounce) bag snack-size Mounds bars, chopped into small, even pieces

### For the Frosting
Pink food coloring

1 (8-ounce) container whipped topping

1 (13.66-ounce) can unsweetened coconut cream, refrigerated

**5** Remove the plastic and gently place the cooled cake on top of the ice cream layer. (If the ice cream layer is too soft to hold the weight of the cake, freeze it for 1 hour more before topping with the cake.) Cover loosely with plastic and freeze for 4 hours or up to 24 hours, until the ice cream layer is fully set.

**6** **Make the frosting:** In a food processor, combine the remaining coconut flakes and 2 drops of pink food coloring. Pulse about 3 times to distribute the food coloring. Add 1 or 2 drops more food coloring and pulse again to intensify the pink color. Set aside.

**7** Scoop the whipped topping into a large bowl. Open the can of chilled coconut cream and use a spoon to scoop the solids from the top into the bowl (reserve the liquid for another use). Beat the mixture with an electric mixer on low speed until well combined.

**8** Remove the cake from the freezer. Remove the springform ring and lift the cake from the pan base onto a serving plate. Use an offset spatula to spread the coconut cream frosting all over the top and sides of the cake, then gently press the pink coconut on top of the frosting. Transfer to the freezer to set for 30 minutes more before slicing and serving.

# FROSTED ANIMAL CRACKER *fudge*

Nothing says "life's too short" like playing with your food. In this recipe, animal crackers, the original play-food, become a rich and satisfying fudge that's almost too fun to eat. (Almost.) The combination of swirls of pink and white fudge, animal crackers on parade, and a final sprinkle of, well, sprinkles makes for the ultimate never-grow-up dessert.

Nonstick cooking spray

14 ounces white chocolate, coarsely chopped

1 (8-ounce) package cream cheese, at room temperature

1 (16-ounce) box powdered sugar

Pink food coloring

1½ cups chopped frosted animal crackers (5 ounces), plus 12 whole crackers for garnish

Nonpareil sprinkles, for topping

**1** Line an 8-inch square baking dish with an 8 by 10-inch piece of parchment paper, leaving a 1-inch overhang on two sides. Coat the parchment and exposed pan sides with nonstick spray.

**2** In a medium microwave-safe bowl, microwave the chocolate on high for about 30 seconds, stirring every 10 seconds, until melted.

**3** In a large bowl using an electric mixer, beat the cream cheese and powdered sugar until well combined, starting on low speed and slowly increasing to high. Pour in the melted chocolate and beat on high speed until the mixture is smooth and fluffy. Transfer about one-quarter of the mixture to a small bowl. Add 2 drops of pink food coloring and whisk to fully incorporate.

**4** Fold the chopped animal crackers into the bowl with the white mixture. Spoon about half of that mixture into the prepared baking dish. Dollop the pink mixture and remaining white mixture over the first white layer, then use a butter knife to swirl the colors. Smooth the top and top with sprinkles. Stand the whole animal crackers upright in four rows of 3 crackers each across the fudge, spacing them evenly. Refrigerate the fudge for about 2 hours, until fully set.

**5** Use the overhanging parchment to transfer the fudge to a cutting board. Cut the fudge into 12 squares with an animal cracker on each square. Serve immediately.

# drink up!

# milkshake OVERLOAD

SERVES 2

1 (5-ounce) box malted milk balls

½ cup hot fudge, at room temperature

1 pint vanilla ice cream

¼ cup Irish cream liqueur (optional)

## Over-the-Toppings

Hot fudge

Marshmallow creme

Donuts

Mini candy bars

Peanut butter cups

Sandwich cookies

Gummy candies

Marshmallows

Popping candies

Dipped pretzels

Frosted animal crackers

Frosted sugar cookies

Sprinkles

Edible glitter

Sparklers

This milkshake contains a whole box of malted milk balls, a whole pint of ice cream, a ton of hot fudge, and a heavy pour of Irish cream liqueur. But that isn't why this recipe is over the top. It's the limitless possibilities for rims, skewers, garnishes, and adornments that take an extraordinary shake and send it soaring. Dip the glass in some hot fudge or marshmallow creme for the perfect base to any rim. Then use wooden skewers to create an endless fantasy of sweet treats floating about the shake. Go ahead, drive it into overload!

**1** Put the malted milk balls in a blender. Blend on high for about 1 minute to pulverize them into coarse crumbs. Add the hot fudge and ice cream and blend again on high for about 1 minute, until everything is thoroughly combined. Add the liqueur (if using) and blend for about 30 seconds to combine.

**2** Pour into two chilled milkshake glasses and add toppings as desired. Serve immediately.

# rainbow kool-aid
## SLUSHIE

**MAKES 2 SLUSHIES**

Part arts and crafts, part delicious slushie. Grab a mixed pack of Kool-Aid for unlimited color combinations or stick to one color to create a beautiful tie-dye swirl around the drink. The possibilities (and flavor combinations) are endless.

**1** Combine the sorbet and vodka in a blender. Blend on high for about 1 minute, until smooth.

**2** Scoop ⅓ cup of the slushie mixture into a tall glass. Add about ⅛ teaspoon of drink mix and stir to combine. Add ⅓ cup more slushie to the glass, then add different colors of drink mix, swirling the colors into a tie-dye pattern, then finish with a final ⅓ cup of the slushie and ⅛ teaspoon drink mix.

**3** Repeat with a second glass, using the remaining slushie mixture. Serve immediately with desired toppings.

1 pint lemon sorbet

¼ cup vodka

Packets of unsweetened drink mix, such as Kool-Aid, in various colors

**Over-the-Toppings**

Edible glitter

Glow sticks

Loop straws

# ITALIAN *cream soda*

Cream and soda don't seem like obvious partners. (Well, except cream soda, but still.) But a fruity, bubbly drink becomes so chic and indulgent with a beautiful swirl of cream. It's a simple touch that suddenly sends it over the top. And when it comes to the fruity, literally any flavor of jam is the right choice for a sweet kick. Don't knock it till you try it!

**1** In a small bowl, whisk together the jam and ¼ cup warm water until well combined. Strain the mixture into a measuring cup. (You should have about ½ cup fruit syrup.)

**2** Divide the ice between two tall glasses. Add ½ cup of the club soda and ¼ cup of the fruit syrup to each glass, then drizzle 2 tablespoons of the cream into each. Add toppings as desired and serve immediately.

## SERVES 2

¼ cup fruit jam

2 cups ice

1 cup club soda

¼ cup heavy cream

### Over-the-Toppings

Gummy fruits

Sour ribbons

Fish-shaped candies

# loaded BLOODY MARY

**For the Infused Vodka**

1 (750 ml) bottle vodka

2 kosher dill pickle spears

¼ cup kosher dill pickle juice

½ jalapeño (cut lengthwise), seeds and all

**For the Bloody Mary Mix**

1 (46-ounce) bottle tomato juice

¼ cup prepared horseradish

¼ cup Worcestershire sauce

¼ cup fresh lime juice

3 tablespoons taco seasoning

**For serving**

Lime wedges, hot sauce, celery salt, crushed nacho cheese-flavored tortilla chips, and ice

**Over-the-Toppings**

Artichoke hearts

Kimchi

Pickle spears

Beef jerky

Stuffed olives

Poached shrimp

Cooked bacon

String cheese

Hard-boiled eggs

Pretzel rods

Celery stalks

The key to this recipe is letting the vodka and the bloody mix chill overnight. The other key is getting all your toppings organized the day before. (Anything cooked will keep in the fridge.) The other-other key is letting everyone build their own bloody. Prep everything before you go out for the night, and in the morning, you'll be ready to host (hangover or not!).

**1** **Make the infused vodka:** Combine the vodka, pickle spears, pickle juice, and jalapeño in a large jar or pitcher. Cover and refrigerate for 12 to 24 hours.

**2** **Make the Bloody Mary mix:** Combine the tomato juice, horseradish, Worcestershire, lime juice, and taco seasoning in another large jar or pitcher. Cover and refrigerate for 12 to 24 hours.

**3** Run a lime wedge around the rim of each glass (or pour hot sauce into a shallow dish and dip the rim of each glass in). Spread celery salt or crushed chips over a shallow dish and dip the rims to coat (or get creative with the rim of your choice!). Fill each glass with ice, then use a shot glass to measure 2 ounces of the infused vodka and 4 ounces of the Bloody Mary mix into each glass. Allow everyone to choose their own toppings.

# COTTON CANDY
 **MAKES 1 DRINK**

This drink is all about a dramatic pour. Load a martini glass with a cloud of cotton candy (pro tip: Stick to a single color for the best effect), then slowly pour the mojito into the glass. Watch as the cocktail and candy melt into one beautiful, vibrant, and very over-the-top cocktail. Sip with caution: This is one dangerous drink!

**1** Combine the mint, sugar, and lime juice in a cocktail shaker, then muddle until the sugar is dissolved (see Note). Add the rum and ice, cover, and shake until the outside of the shaker is frosted. Add the club soda to the shaker.

**2** Pull a large piece of cotton candy to dramatically fill a martini glass with a wispy shape. Slowly strain the cocktail over the cotton candy, add any desired finishing touches, and serve immediately.

## NOTE
Muddling is a cocktail technique to gently release oils from herbs. If you have a cocktail set, the thick wooden dowel is called a muddler. (The handle of a thick wooden spoon also works!) Don't slam the muddler in there and start attacking. Press on the herbs and twist gently to release their oils while keeping the leaves mostly intact.

4 sprigs of mint

½ teaspoon sugar

2 tablespoons fresh lime juice

2 ounces white rum

1 cup ice

2 ounces club soda

Cotton candy

### Over-the-Toppings
Glow sticks

Loop straws

Edible luster spray for the glass

# campfire FLOAT

**MAKES 1 DRINK**

½ cup crushed graham crackers

Marshmallow creme, such as Fluff

Hot fudge

2 jumbo marshmallows

2 scoops chocolate ice cream

1 ounce spiced rum (optional)

Vanilla-flavored cola, as desired

### Over-the-Toppings

Striped straws

Color-changing spoons

Flavored marshmallows

All the flavor of everyone's favorite campfire treat, with a little fizzy cola to wash it down. Toasted marshmallows, chocolate ice cream, and a graham cracker–marshmallow rim all mingle with vanilla cola for the rush of the outdoors, but indoors. It's so delicious, you'll be dying for s'more.

**1** Sprinkle the crushed graham crackers on a small plate. Dip the rim of a milkshake glass (or other tall glass) directly into the container of marshmallow creme, then dip it in the graham crackers. Drizzle hot fudge all over the inside of the glass. Set the glass in the freezer while you toast the marshmallows.

**2** Place the marshmallows on a wooden skewer. Hold the skewer over a stovetop burner on high heat, rotating it to toast and char the marshmallows in places. Slide one marshmallow into the bottom of the prepared glass. Keep the other marshmallow on the skewer and set aside.

**3** Add the ice cream to the glass, then add the rum (if using). Top off with vanilla cola. Trim the skewer with the toasted marshmallow to be slightly wider than the glass and rest the skewer over the glass. Serve immediately with toppings and decorations, as desired.

# SANGRIA *iced tea*

Pour, stir, chill, and sip. That's all it takes to build a sangria that's light on effort, but big on flavor. Hibiscus tea gives the sauv blanc a stunning red color, while ginger and mango accent the wine's fruit flavors. A can of fruit cocktail is a sensible shortcut, but feel free to sub in two cups of bite-size fresh fruit!

**1** In a large pitcher, combine the boiling water and sugar and stir until the sugar has dissolved. Add the tea bags and let steep for 30 minutes. Discard the tea bags.

**2** Add the sauvignon blanc, the fruit cocktail and its syrup, the kombucha, hard seltzer, and lemon juice to the pitcher. Stir to combine, then cover in plastic wrap and refrigerate for at least 1 hour or up to 4 hours.

**3** To serve, fill a large pitcher or jar with ice and ladle in the sangria and fruit. Serve with finishing touches.

## SERVES 8 TO 10

1 cup boiling water

½ cup sugar

4 hibiscus tea bags

1 (750 ml) bottle sauvignon blanc

2 (8.5-ounce) cans fruit cocktail

1 (16-ounce) bottle ginger kombucha

1 (12-ounce) can mango-flavored hard seltzer

¼ cup fresh lemon juice

### Over-the-Toppings

Edible flower ice cubes

Cocktail umbrellas

Watermelon slices

### Ice, Ice, Baby

Ice cubes in fun shapes are the easiest way to perk up any drink. But even a standard ice cube tray can be transformed with a few easy hacks. For clear ice, boil distilled water for 10 minutes, then cover with a lid and let cool to room temperature, about 1 hour. Fill an ice cube tray with edible flowers, berries, or fruit slices, then slowly pour the cooled distilled water over the top. Freeze until solid. For flavored ice cubes, add a tea bag or fruit juice to the water after it has boiled. (Remember, alcohol doesn't freeze!)

# electric LEMONADE

2 cups sugar

¼ cup butterfly pea flower tea (see page 11)

2 cups fresh lemon juice

### Over-the-Toppings

Light-up ice cubes

Glow sticks

Edible glitter for the rim

Butterfly pea tea, an herbal tea made from the petals of the blue butterfly pea flower, is nature's little magic trick. When steeped in hot water, the buds make a royal blue tea. But when something acidic like lemon hits the tea, it turns a beautiful lavender. The best way to serve this drink is with the blue tea in the glass and the lemon juice in a small glass on the side; pour the lemon over the tea, and watch the magic unfold in real time.

**1** In a small saucepan, combine the sugar and 2 cups water and bring to boil over high heat, stirring occasionally. Once the sugar has dissolved, remove from the heat and add the tea. Let the syrup cool completely, about 1 hour, then scoop out and discard the tea.

**2** Divide the lemon juice evenly among four small glasses. Fill four tall glasses with ice and add ¾ cup of the tea syrup to each glass. Add toppings and decorations to the tall glasses and serve with the lemon juice on the side, allowing each person to add it themselves to create their own alchemy.

# chile
# PINEAPPLE WHIP

SERVES 2

Popular in a certain theme park, this whip is like soft-serve gone wild. Since we use fresh pineapple to make the whip, it makes sense to put the scooped-out pineapple shell to good use as the most over-the-top cup. After freezing the pineapple pieces, it's just a quick whir in the blender. (Of course you can make life easier and simply buy frozen pineapple chunks and use milkshake glasses instead of the shell.) A splash of rum is optional, but it's the chili powder that really sends this into the stratosphere. This has to be the best way to enjoy a piña, colada or not.

**1** Slice the top 2 inches off the pineapple. Use a pineapple corer (or sharp knife) to remove the fruit. Cut off and discard the core. Wrap the pineapple shell in plastic wrap and refrigerate.

**2** Cut the pineapple into chunks until you have 4 cups. (Reserve the remaining pineapple for another use.) Spread the pineapple on a rimmed baking sheet lined with parchment paper. Freeze for 12 to 24 hours.

**3** Pour the condensed coconut milk into a blender. Add the frozen pineapple and blend on high speed for about 1 minute, scraping down the sides as needed, until the mixture is smooth and resembles the texture of whipped cream. Scoop the whip into a piping bag fitted with a wide tip (or see page 35). Set the bag upright in a large glass and transfer the bag to the freezer for 15 minutes.

*recipe continues*

1 (3- to 4-pound) pineapple

1 (11.25-ounce) can sweetened condensed coconut milk

2 ounces spiced rum (optional)

Chili powder, for garnish

### Over-the-Toppings

Edible luster spray for the pineapple shell

Loop straws

Color-changing spoons

**4** Remove the pineapple shell from the refrigerator and unwrap it. Pour in the rum (if using) and swirl the pineapple to coat the interior. Remove the bag with the pineapple whip from the freezer and pipe the whip into the pineapple shell. Dust with chili powder and serve immediately, with edible straws, color-changing spoons, and other decorations as desired.

# HOT BUTTERED RUM
## cider  **MAKES 1 DRINK**

A heavily spiced apple cider goes straight to the heart of cozy sweater weather. A hot buttered rum warms you from the core in the coldest months. When the two drinks combine, you have the comfy-coziest sip possible.

**1** **Make the spiced butter:** In a medium bowl, combine the butter, sugar, salt, cinnamon, allspice, ginger, cloves, nutmeg, and cayenne and stir until well combined. Scoop the butter into an airtight container. Store in the refrigerator for up to 1 week.

**2** **Make the cider:** In a small saucepan, combine the cider and 1 tablespoon of the spiced butter. Bring to a simmer over medium-low heat, then cook, stirring occasionally to melt the butter, for about 5 minutes.

**3** Pour the cider into a mug and add the rum. Serve immediately, with desired toppings.

*For the Spiced Butter*
½ cup (1 stick) unsalted butter, at room temperature

¼ cup (packed) light brown sugar

½ teaspoon kosher salt

½ teaspoon ground cinnamon

½ teaspoon ground allspice

½ teaspoon ground ginger

¼ teaspoon ground cloves

¼ teaspoon ground nutmeg

⅛ teaspoon cayenne pepper

*For the Cider*
1 cup apple cider

2 ounces spiced rum

**Over-the-Toppings**

Powdered donuts

Orange peel studded with cloves

Whipped cream

# SALTED CARAMEL

 **SERVES 1**

Caramel sauce

Flaky sea salt

1 scoop vanilla ice cream

1 ounce strong brewed coffee
(about 1 espresso)

1 ounce Irish cream liqueur,
coffee liqueur, or almond
liqueur

**Over-the-Toppings**

Crushed graham
crackers

Chocolate-filled rolled
wafer cookies

Whipped cream

Affogato, an Italian concoction of gelato and espresso, sits somewhere between drink and dessert. To send this very adult treat over the top, a splash of liqueur and a generous drizzle of salted caramel hit all the right spots.

Drizzle an ice cream bowl or large coffee cup with caramel sauce. Sprinkle a small amount of flaky salt over the caramel. Add the ice cream to the bowl or coffee cup, then pour in the coffee and liqueur. Drizzle more caramel over the ice cream and sprinkle with more salt. Serve immediately, with desired toppings.

# WATERMELON MARGARITA
## *party punch*

The hardest part about this punch is cutting a watermelon. From there it's just a few scoops, a whirl in the blender, and a couple of over-the-top decorations. Equally refreshing with or without tequila, it's the easiest way to tell a crowd "It's time to party!"

**1** Cut about 2 inches off one long side of the watermelon (not the top or the bottom; for an even more over-the-top presentation, cut in a zigzag pattern). Use a large metal spoon to scoop out all the fruit; set the shell aside and cut the fruit into chunks. Transfer 3 cups of the fruit to a blender and reserve the rest for another use.

**2** Add the tequila, lime juice, sugar, mint, and jalapeño to the blender. Blend on high for about 1 minute to make a smooth drink with flecks of mint and jalapeño.

**3** Pour the margarita into the watermelon shell. Finish with the decorations of your choice. To serve, fill six glasses with ice and ladle the margarita into each. Garnish each glass with a mint sprig and serve immediately.

1 (8-pound) seedless watermelon

1½ cups tequila blanco

1 cup fresh lime juice (from about 8 limes)

1 cup sugar

½ cup fresh mint leaves

½ jalapeño, seeded

Ice and mint sprigs, for serving

### *Over-the-Toppings*

Sparklers

Flamingo picks

Cocktail umbrellas

# HONEY BEAR
## *horchata*  SERVES 2

Honey

1 cup vanilla rice milk

1 cup vanilla rice-based ice cream

1 teaspoon ground cinnamon

2 ounces spiced rum (optional)

### Over-the-Toppings

Edible luster spray for the bears

Striped straws

Fresh honeycomb

Horchata, a popular Mexican drink, is a milky beverage made from ground rice and water with plenty of cinnamon. For an icy variation, rice milk and ice cream jump into the blender with cinnamon and an optional splash of rum. Serving in empty honey bottles is not required; even in a regular glass, this is still an adorable drink to share with your honey bear.

**1** Drizzle honey on the inside of two cleaned-out honey bears. Set aside.

**2** In a blender, combine the rice milk, ice cream, and cinnamon and blend on high speed for about 1 minute, until smooth. Add the rum (if using) and blend for about 30 seconds more to combine.

**3** Pour the horchata into the prepared honey bears. Serve immediately, with toppings and decorations as desired.

# nibbles & bits

# SANDIA loca

The name of this dish translates to "crazy watermelon" (well, literally "watermelon crazy," because that's how Spanish works), and nothing has ever been more correct. It's a fruit salad that has absolutely 100% lost its mind. An innocent watermelon gets loaded with piles of fruit, candy, chili powder, and a quick homemade chamoy, aka the best sweet-spicy-sour sauce around.

**1 Make the chamoy:** In a medium bowl, whisk together the apricot jam, plum jam, chili powder, and lime juice. Press the mixture through a fine-mesh strainer set over a small bowl and set aside. Discard any solids left in the strainer.

**2 Prep the watermelon:** Cut about ¼ inch off one side of the watermelon to create a flat surface. Cut about 4 inches off the opposite side. (For an even more over-the-top presentation, cut in a zigzag pattern.) Scoop out some of the flesh with a melon baller and set aside. Use a large spoon to scoop out the remaining flesh and cut it into chunks. Transfer the chunks to the hollowed-out watermelon. Reserve any extra flesh for another use.

**3** Drizzle some of the chamoy over the filled watermelon, then sprinkle some chili-lime seasoning over the top. Start piling on the toppings, drizzling with chamoy and sprinkling with chili-lime seasoning as you go. Serve immediately.

### For the Chamoy
1 (13-ounce) jar apricot jam (a heaping 1 cup)

1 (13-ounce) jar plum jam (a heaping 1 cup)

½ cup chili powder

¼ cup fresh lime juice

### For the Watermelon
1 (15- to 20-pound) watermelon

Chili-lime seasoning

### Over-the-Toppings
Watermelon balls

Cantaloupe balls

Honeydew balls

Kiwi stars

Mango slices

Blueberries

Strawberries

Oranges

Limes

Gummy fruit candies

Popping candies

Sour ribbons

Fish-shaped candies

Lollipops

Tamarind straws

Spicy rolled tortilla chips

Japanese-style peanuts

Mexican spaghetti candy

Cocktail umbrellas

Rainbow sparklers

# HONEY MUSTARD STUFFED *giant pretzel*

**SERVES 8**

1½ teaspoons sugar

1¼ teaspoons active dry yeast

2¼ cups all-purpose flour, plus more for dusting

1½ teaspoons kosher salt

2 tablespoons olive oil

4 ounces cream cheese, at room temperature

2 tablespoons grainy Dijon mustard

1 tablespoon yellow mustard

4 teaspoons honey

2 tablespoons unsalted butter, melted

1 cup crushed honey mustard-flavored pretzels

The best dip for pretzel sticks is honey mustard, no argument. But haven't we all wished that dip could somehow be the gooey insides of a giant soft pretzel? Sure we have! And today is the day that wish becomes reality. Honey. Two mustards. Cream cheese. A comically large, homemade doughy-soft pretzel. Those addictive honey mustard pretzels crushed on top. This pretzel has it all, and you'll love every bite.

**1** In a large bowl, whisk the sugar with ¾ cup warm water. Add the yeast and let stand for 5 minutes, until the mixture is cloudy at the surface.

**2** Add the flour, salt, and 1 tablespoon of the oil to the yeast mixture. Use a wooden spoon to mix thoroughly until the dough comes together into a firm ball. Remove the dough from the bowl momentarily, grease the bowl with the remaining 1 tablespoon oil, and return the dough to the bowl. Cover with a clean dish towel or plastic wrap and let sit in a warm place for 1 hour, until the dough has doubled in size.

**3** Preheat the oven to 400°F and set a rack in the center. Line a baking sheet with parchment paper.

**4** In a small bowl, use a fork to mix the cream cheese, grainy mustard, yellow mustard, and honey into a smooth paste. Set aside.

*recipe continues*

5 Turn the dough out onto a lightly floured surface. Using your fingers or a rolling pin, stretch and flatten the dough into a long, thin strip, about 30 inches long and 4 inches wide. Spread the cream cheese mixture lengthwise down the center of the dough strip, leaving a 1-inch border at the top and bottom. Bring the long sides of the dough together to enclose the filling, then fold and pinch the seam to seal; pinch the ends to seal as well. Turn the filled dough seam-side down and roll it slightly to seal and lengthen it back to 30 inches.

6 Carefully form the filled rope of dough into a pretzel shape: Holding the ends, form a "U" shape, then twist the ends around each other and connect them to the bottom of the "U." Transfer the pretzel to the prepared baking sheet and bake for 25 to 30 minutes, until golden brown.

7 Brush the pretzel with the melted butter, then sprinkle the crushed pretzels over the top and press them gently to adhere. Serve immediately.

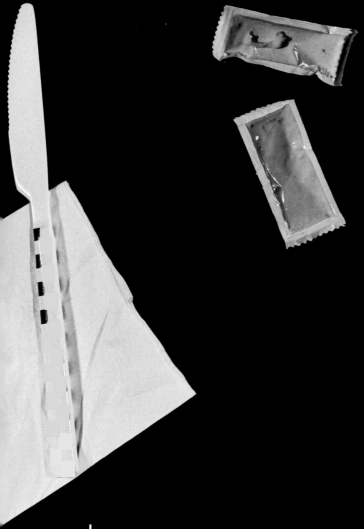

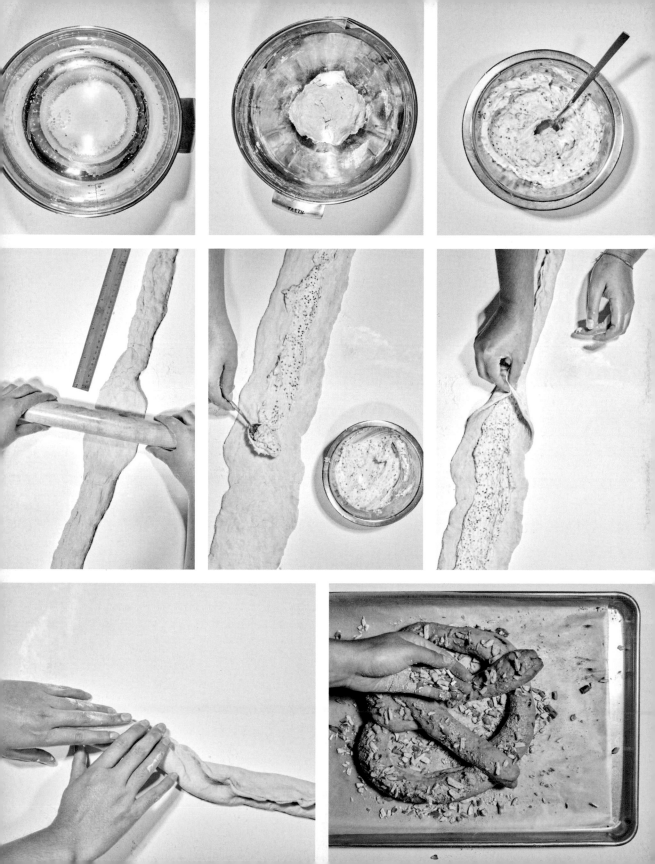

# ranch popcorn CHEX MIX

**SERVES 10**

2 cups wheat squares cereal, such as Wheat Chex

2 cups corn squares cereal, such as Corn Chex

2 cups rice squares cereal, such as Rice Chex

2 cups mini pretzels

2 cups bagel chips

2 cups raw mixed nuts

½ cup (1 stick) unsalted butter

2 (1-ounce) packets ranch seasoning

1 (6¾-ounce) bag white cheddar popcorn

For every ranch dressing addict (basically everyone), this is the snack you deserve. All the usual suspects of a great Chex mix—including the real stars, bagel chips—get tossed in ranch seasoning and then toasted. Then, to amp up the savory crunch, white cheddar popcorn joins the party. It just makes sense.

**1** Preheat the oven to 250°F and set a rack in the center.

**2** In a large bowl, combine the cereals, pretzels, bagel chips, and nuts.

**3** In a small skillet, melt the butter over low heat, then remove from the heat and whisk in the ranch seasoning. Drizzle the ranch butter over the cereal mixture and toss to coat.

**4** Spread the mixture over a rimmed baking sheet and bake for 1 hour, stirring every 15 minutes. Let cool on the baking sheet for 30 minutes, then transfer to a large bowl and add the popcorn. Toss to combine and serve immediately, or store in an airtight container at room temperature for up to 2 weeks . . . if it lasts that long!

# EVERYTHING BAGEL
## cornbread
## squares

**MAKES 9 SQUARES**

From the outside this might look like a simple cornbread with everything bagel seasoning on top. Fun, but kind of whatever, right? One bite of the scallion cream cheese hiding inside, and you'll see why this earns the over-the-top medal. It's a perfect savory bite to accompany drinks, dinner, or even brunch.

**1** Preheat the oven to 400°F and set a rack in the center. Coat an 8-inch square baking dish with nonstick spray.

**2** In a small saucepan, melt the butter over low heat. Remove from the heat and add the milk and lemon juice. Set aside.

**3** In a large bowl, whisk together the cornmeal, flour, sugar, baking powder, baking soda, and salt until combined. Add the eggs and the milk mixture and whisk to incorporate, being careful not to overmix (it's okay if the mixture is slightly lumpy). Add the cream cheese and scallions and use a silicone spatula to gently fold them into the batter, keeping the cubes of cream cheese intact.

**4** Pour the mixture into the prepared baking dish and smooth the top. Sprinkle the everything bagel seasoning over the top. Bake for about 20 minutes, until a toothpick inserted into the center comes out clean. Let cool completely in the pan before slicing into 9 pieces and serving.

Nonstick cooking spray

½ cup (1 stick) unsalted butter

1 cup whole milk

1 tablespoon fresh lemon juice

1½ cups yellow cornmeal

1 cup all-purpose flour

2 tablespoons sugar

1 teaspoon baking powder

1 teaspoon baking soda

1 teaspoon kosher salt

3 large eggs

1 (8-ounce) package cream cheese, cut into ½-inch cubes

4 scallions, thinly sliced

3 tablespoons everything bagel seasoning

# DORITOS NACHOS *tower*

**SERVES 4**

1 red onion, coarsely chopped

½ cup white vinegar

1 tablespoon olive oil

1 (14-ounce) package extra-firm tofu, drained and patted dry, or 1 pound ground meat of your choice

Kosher salt and freshly ground black pepper

"Why are the nachos vertical?" you might ask. This book is called *Over the Top,* we'll remind you. Save the logic for other cookbooks and just trust us that a pile of Doritos blanketed in cheese sauce, stacked with savory crumbles, and stuffed with beans is exactly the way nachos should be now and forever.

**1** Use a can opener to cut off the lip at the top of the coffee can, then cut open the bottom of the can. Place the resulting cylinder on a serving plate and set aside.

**2** Combine the onion and vinegar in a small bowl. Set aside.

**3** In a large skillet, heat the oil over medium-high heat. When the oil is shimmering, add the tofu and use a wooden spoon to break it into small pieces. Season well with salt and pepper. Cook, continuing to break apart the tofu so it resembles the texture of ground meat, for about 5 minutes, until the tofu has lost some of its moisture. (If using ground meat, cook for 5 to 10 minutes, until cooked through.) Add the salsa verde and simmer for 5 minutes, until slightly reduced. Remove from the heat and stir in the cilantro. Set aside.

**4** While the tofu cooks, combine the American cheese and milk in a small saucepan. Cook over low heat, whisking occasionally, for about 5 minutes, until the cheese has fully melted and the mixture is smooth. Set the sauce aside.

**5** Drain the onion. Add a layer of chips to the prepared coffee can and press them against the plate at the bottom, breaking them into coarse pieces. Add one-third of the tofu mixture, black beans, cheese sauce, and onion to the can. Add another layer of chips, press down, and repeat with another third of the tofu, beans, sauce, and onion. Continue with the remaining ingredients to fill the can, pressing down to compact the layers.

**6** Slowly lift the coffee can to reveal the nacho tower. Serve immediately, with bowls of salsa, guacamole, and salsa con queso alongside.

1 (16-ounce) jar salsa verde

½ cup coarsely chopped fresh cilantro leaves

12 slices yellow American cheese

½ cup whole milk

1 (9.75-ounce) bag nacho cheese–flavored tortilla chips, such as Doritos

1 (15.5-ounce) can black beans, drained and rinsed

Salsa, guacamole, and salsa con queso, for serving

*Special Equipment*
Empty 20- to 30-ounce coffee tin, rinsed and dried

# HUSH PUPPY
## *jalapeño poppers*

The vibe of this dish is very "all your favorite apps in one bite." Think mozzarella sticks plus jalapeño poppers plus hush pups . . . yeah, kinda the best thing ever. Who needs a sampler platter when you have a plate of these at the melty ready?

**1** In a large bowl, whisk together the corn muffin mix, egg, milk, flour, salt, and pepper. Cover and refrigerate for 30 minutes (the batter will thicken).

**2** Meanwhile, slice the string cheese sticks in half crosswise to create 12 pieces total. Slice the top ¼ inch off the stem end of the jalapeños and discard. Use the handle of a soup spoon to scrape out the seeds and ribs from the jalapeños, leaving the shell of the chile intact. Insert one piece of string cheese into each jalapeño. Cover and refrigerate while the batter rests.

**3** In a Dutch oven, heat the oil over medium-high heat until it reaches 350°F on an instant-read thermometer. Working in batches, use tongs to coat the jalapeños in the batter, then transfer to the hot oil and fry for about 4 minutes, flipping them occasionally to ensure an even golden brown color all over. Transfer the poppers to a wire rack or a paper towel–lined plate to drain. Repeat to fry the remaining poppers. Let cool for about 5 minutes, then serve, with marinara, tartar sauce, and salsa con queso for dipping.

1 (8.5-ounce) box corn muffin mix

1 large egg

1 cup whole milk

¼ cup all-purpose flour

½ teaspoon kosher salt

½ teaspoon freshly ground black pepper

6 sticks string cheese

12 jalapeños

4 cups vegetable oil

Marinara sauce, tartar sauce, and salsa con queso, for serving

# SEVEN-LAYER DIP—
## dip & chips

SERVES 8

8 (6-inch) corn tortillas

2 tablespoons olive oil

2 tablespoons taco seasoning

1 (12-ounce) jar red pepper jelly

1 (8-ounce) package cream cheese, at room temperature

1 (16-ounce) package guacamole

1 (15-ounce) jar French onion dip

1 (16-ounce) jar black bean dip

1 (15-ounce) jar salsa con queso

1 (16-ounce) bottle ranch dressing

1 (15-ounce) container pico de gallo

Why complicate things when you can have it all? That's our mantra in life and our mantra in dips. Seven all-stars—everything from guac to ranch dressing—line up for a deep-dive of a dip. Work down layer by layer, or head straight to the bottom, scooping up (ready for this?) red pepper jelly, guacamole, French onion dip, black bean dip, salsa con queso, ranch dressing, and pico de gallo (!!!) on the way up. It's a mix of savory and sweet that hits in all the right ways. Oh, and speaking of the chips, some homemade oven-baked tortilla chips with taco seasoning are just the ticket for a perfect crunch. Or just grab a bag of your favorite tortilla chips and go to town.

**1** Preheat the oven to 350°F and set two racks in the upper and lower thirds.

**2** Stack the tortillas on a cutting board and cut them into eighths (like a pizza). Transfer to a large bowl, add the oil and taco seasoning, and toss to coat.

**3** Spread the seasoned tortilla pieces in a single layer over two rimmed baking sheets, arranging them in 4 rows of 8 pieces on each sheet and making sure there's no overlap. Bake for 20 to 25 minutes, until the chips are crisp and golden brown, rotating the pans and swapping their positions in the oven halfway through. Let cool completely on the baking sheets.

**4** While the chips bake, in a small bowl, whisk together the jelly and cream cheese. Spread the mixture in an even layer over the bottom of a large dip bowl. Spread the guacamole over the top, then the French onion dip, creating smooth layers. Spoon in the black bean dip, then the queso. Pour over the ranch, then spoon in the pico as the final layer. Cover and refrigerate for at least 30 minutes and up to 4 hours. Serve the dip with the chips alongside.

# SPINACH & ARTICHOKE
## baked brie

1 tablespoon olive oil

2 garlic cloves, thinly sliced

1 (10-ounce) package frozen spinach, thawed and drained

1 (8.46-ounce) can artichoke hearts, drained

¼ cup shredded mozzarella cheese

¼ cup grated Parmesan cheese

2 tablespoons sour cream

2 tablespoons mayonnaise

½ teaspoon kosher salt

¼ teaspoon freshly ground black pepper

¼ teaspoon red pepper flakes

1 sheet frozen puff pastry, thawed

All-purpose flour, for dusting

1 (8-ounce) wheel Brie

1 large egg

½ cup shredded cheddar cheese

1 teaspoon finely chopped fresh chives

Crackers, for serving

At this point, why not. If you've made it this far into the book, you get that over the top = pure pleasure. Baked Brie is the warm and gooey appetizer dreams are made of, which happens to be the same description for spinach-and-artichoke dip. So really . . . why not bring the two together! Pile a cheesy, garlicky dip on top of a wheel of Brie. Wrap it in puff pastry and bake until golden and flaky. Then put politeness aside and attack it with knives, spoons, and crackers until you sit back in bliss.

**1** Preheat the oven to 375°F and set a rack in the center. Line a rimmed baking sheet with parchment paper.

**2** In a large skillet, heat the oil over medium heat. When the oil is shimmering, add the garlic and sauté for about 4 minutes, until soft and fragrant. Add the spinach, artichokes, mozzarella, Parmesan, sour cream, mayonnaise, salt, black pepper, and red pepper flakes. Cook, stirring occasionally, for about 4 minutes, until the cheese has melted and the mixture is thick and steaming hot.

**3** While the filling cooks, lay the puff pastry on a lightly floured work surface. Roll it into a 14-inch square, then transfer it to the prepared baking sheet. Set the wheel of Brie in the center of the pastry square and spread the spinach-artichoke mixture over and around the Brie.

**4** Bring the corners of the pastry square together to enclose the filling, then pinch the seams to seal. Whisk the egg with 1 tablespoon water to make an egg wash, then brush it all over the pastry. Pile the cheddar over the top and bake for about 30 minutes, until the pastry is puffed and golden. Sprinkle with the chives and serve immediately, with a cheese knife and crackers.

# cheesy FRITO PIE dip

Why hoard a tiny bag of Frito pie when you can just cut open a big bag and make it a social event? Unlike the traditional recipe, these chips get crushed and layered in with a warm, cheesy, vegetarian (shh!) bean dip. A bunch of fresh elements cover the top (plus more cheese, obviously). From there, the tortilla chips are on the table and it's everyone for themselves. It's the dip that won't quit.

**1** Use a sharp paring knife to cut a large rectangle out of the front of the bag of corn chips to create a bowl, leaving a 1-inch border. Pour the chips into a large zip top freezer bag, seal, and crush into small pieces.

**2** In a medium saucepan, combine the vinegar, sugar, salt, and ¼ cup water and bring to a boil over medium-high heat, stirring to dissolve the sugar and salt. Remove from the heat and add the jalapeño and onion. Set aside.

**3** **Make the dip:** In a medium saucepan, heat the oil over medium-high heat. When the oil shimmers, add the tomato paste and taco seasoning. Cook, stirring occasionally, for about 2 minutes, until the paste is soft and the seasoning is fragrant. Add the beans, salt, and beer and stir to combine. Let the mixture come to a boil, then cover and reduce the heat to medium-low. Simmer for about 10 minutes, until the beans are soft and the mixture is thick. Remove from the heat and use a wooden spoon to stir and mash most of the beans (some whole beans are fine) until the dip is very thick. Add the cheese and stir to melt.

**4** Spread 1½ cups of the crushed Fritos over the bottom of the bag bowl. Spread the dip over the top, pushing it into the corners of the bag with a spoon. Top with the remaining crushed Fritos. Add the tomato. Drain the onion and jalapeño and pile them over the tomatoes. Sprinkle the cheese over the top, then dollop with the sour cream. Finish with the chives and serve immediately, with tortilla chips for scooping.

## SERVES 6

1 (9¼-ounce) bag fried corn chips, such as Fritos

¼ cup distilled white vinegar

1 teaspoon sugar

1 teaspoon kosher salt

1 jalapeño, stemmed, seeded, and finely chopped

½ red onion, finely chopped

*For the Dip*

1 tablespoon olive oil

1 (6-ounce) can tomato paste

2 tablespoons taco seasoning

1 (15.5 ounce) can pinto beans, drained and rinsed

½ teaspoon kosher salt

1 (12-ounce) can lager beer

¼ cup shredded cheddar cheese

1 plum tomato, finely chopped

½ cup shredded cheddar cheese

¼ cup sour cream

1 tablespoon minced fresh chives

Tortilla chips, for serving

# flaming-hot ELOTE

Elote is perfect on its own. But corn chips *on* corn is the move of the century. For those in the dark, elote is Mexican-style corn on the cob. Grilled, slathered in mayo and cotija cheese, and dusted with chili powder, it's about as close to perfect as a vegetable can get. Here we swap out the chili powder for a bag of crushed-up Flamin' Hot Cheetos, which adds a bonus round of savory corn flavor and an addictive level of spice. Get 'em while they're hot!

4 ears of corn, husks on

¼ cup mayonnaise

5 tablespoons crumbled cotija cheese

1 (8.5-ounce) bag flaming-hot cheese snacks, such as Flamin' Hot Cheetos

1 tablespoon olive oil

1 lime, quartered, for serving

**1** Soak the ears of corn in a large bowl of water for 30 minutes.

**2** While the corn soaks, heat a grill to medium-high or heat a grill pan over medium-high heat. When the grill is hot, remove the ears of corn from the water and lay them (still in their husks) on the grill or grill pan. Grill for about 5 minutes on each side, until the husks have grill marks all over. Transfer the corn to a plate to cool for about 10 minutes.

**3** Meanwhile, in a small bowl, stir together the mayonnaise and 3 tablespoons of the cotija. Set aside.

**4** Pour the cheese snacks into a food processor and process for about 30 seconds, until broken down into coarse crumbs. Pour onto a large plate and set aside.

**5** When the corn is cool enough to handle, peel back the husks, leaving them attached at the base of the corncob. Remove and discard the silks. Remove one layer of husk from each ear of corn and tie it around the husk, creating a tail on the corn. Repeat with the other ears.

**6** Brush the ears of corn all over with the oil and set them back on the grill. Grill for about 3 minutes on each side, until they have char marks all over.

**7** Transfer the corn to a plate and immediately brush with the mayo-cheese mixture. Roll the ears over the crushed cheese snacks to coat thoroughly, pressing to adhere the crumbs to the corn. Stack the corn on a plate and sprinkle the remaining 2 tablespoons cotija over the top. Serve immediately, with the lime wedges.

# PLENTY
## of fish

This isn't a cheese board. This isn't chips and dips. This isn't even a thoughtful charcuterie platter. This is the big leagues, the real deal, the over-the-top of over-the-top. In other words, this spread of seafood is only for people you really, *really* like. Pick and choose a few of the recipes below based on your budget, or go big and lay out the whole shebang. Bubble machine and whale sounds optional, but highly recommended.

# CLAMS CASINO

24 littleneck clams (about 2 pounds)

4 cups kosher salt, plus more as needed

2 tablespoons unsalted butter

4 slices thick-cut bacon, diced

2 garlic cloves, minced

½ cup dried bread crumbs

1 tablespoon grated Parmesan cheese

Freshly ground black pepper

1 tablespoon minced fresh parsley leaves

**1** Place the clams in a large bowl of salted water and soak for 30 minutes to release any grit and sand. Carefully lift the clams from the bowl, without disturbing the sediment at the bottom, and scrub them under running water.

**2** Fill a large pot with 2 inches of water and bring to a boil over high heat. Add the clams, cover, and cook for about 5 minutes, until the clams open. Drain the clams and discard any unopened ones. Set aside.

**3** In a large skillet, melt the butter over medium heat. Add the bacon and sauté, stirring occasionally, for about 5 minutes, until crisp and golden. Add the garlic and sauté, stirring, for about 1 minute more, until fragrant. Remove from the heat and stir in the bread crumbs and Parmesan. Season with salt and pepper.

**4** Preheat the broiler to high and set a rack 6 inches from the broiler heat source.

**5** Cover a rimmed baking sheet with the 4 cups of salt. Discard the empty shell halves and nestle the clams in the salt to hold them steady. Spoon the bread crumb mixture over the clams. Transfer to the oven and broil for 2 to 3 minutes, until the bread crumbs are toasted. Garnish with the parsley.

# MUSSELS

1 pound mussels

Kosher salt

1 tablespoon olive oil

1 small shallot, minced

2 garlic cloves, minced

2 sprigs of thyme

¼ cup dry white wine

1 lemon, halved

1 tablespoon unsalted butter

2 tablespoons minced fresh parsley leaves

**1** Place the mussels in a large bowl of salted water and soak for 30 minutes to release any grit and sand. Carefully lift the mussels from the bowl, without disturbing the sediment on the bottom, and scrub them under running water. Pull off and discard any beards.

**2** In a large pot, heat the oil over medium heat. When the oil is shimmering, add the shallot, garlic, and thyme. Sauté, stirring occasionally, for about 5 minutes, until the shallot has softened. Add the mussels and stir to coat. Add the wine and squeeze the juice from the lemon halves into the pot. Bring the liquid to a simmer, then cover the pot. Simmer the mussels for about 5 minutes, until the shells open.

**3** Remove from the heat and discard any unopened mussels. Add the butter and parsley and stir to coat.

## CAJUN SHRIMP

1 pound shrimp, peeled (tails removed) and deveined

1 red bell pepper, diced

1 andouille sausage, sliced in ¼-inch pieces

1 tablespoon olive oil

Kosher salt and freshly ground black pepper

1 teaspoon smoked paprika

1 teaspoon garlic powder

½ teaspoon onion powder

½ teaspoon dried oregano

½ teaspoon red pepper flakes

½ teaspoon cayenne pepper

1 Preheat the oven to 400°F and set a rack in the center.

2 Arrange the shrimp, bell pepper, and sausage on a rimmed baking sheet. Drizzle with the oil, season with salt and black pepper, and toss to coat. Roast for about 10 minutes, until the shrimp are deeply pink.

3 Meanwhile, in a medium serving bowl, whisk together the paprika, garlic powder, onion powder, oregano, red pepper flakes, and cayenne.

4 Add the shrimp, bell pepper, and sausage to the spice mixture and toss to coat.

## WASABI TUNA SALAD

2 (5-ounce) cans tuna (water- or oil-packed)

¼ cup mayonnaise

1 teaspoon wasabi paste

1 teaspoon rice vinegar

Juice of ½ lime

1 (0.6-ounce) package seaweed snacks, stacked and thinly sliced

1 tablespoon toasted sesame seeds

Drain the tuna and transfer it to a medium bowl. Add the mayonnaise, wasabi, vinegar, lime juice, and seaweed. Stir to combine, then top with the sesame seeds.

*recipes continue*

## SHRIMP COCKTAIL

1 lemon, halved

2 sprigs of parsley

1 tablespoon kosher salt

1 tablespoon whole
black peppercorns

1 pound shrimp, peeled
(tails left on) and
deveined

½ cup cocktail sauce

**1** Fill a large pot with water. Squeeze the juice from the lemon halves into the pot, then drop in the juiced lemon. Add the parsley, salt, and peppercorns. Bring to a boil over high heat, then remove from the heat. Add the shrimp and poach for about 3 minutes, until deeply pink and coiled.

**2** Transfer the shrimp to a bowl of ice water (if making the lobster tails and/or boiled potatoes, reserve the poaching liquid) and set aside for up to 1 hour, then drain. (If you won't be serving the shrimp immediately, wrap in a damp paper towel and store in a zip-top bag in the refrigerator for up to 2 days.) Serve with the cocktail sauce in a bowl alongside.

## LOBSTER TAILS

4 lobster tails

4 tablespoons (½ stick)
unsalted butter

**1** Return the poaching liquid you used to cook the shrimp to a boil, then add the lobster tails. Boil for about 5 minutes, until the tails are deep red and an instant-read thermometer inserted into the center of a tail reads 140°F. Transfer the lobster to a bowl of ice water. Reserve the pot of water.

**2** In a microwave-safe dipping bowl, microwave the butter on high for about 30 seconds, until melted. Serve the lobster tails with the melted butter alongside.

## POTATOES, SOFT-BOILED EGGS, AND CORN

½ pound fingerling or new potatoes

6 large eggs

4 ears of corn, husked and halved

Return the cooking liquid from the shrimp and lobster to a boil and add the potatoes. Cook for 3 minutes, then add the eggs and cook for 2 minutes more. Add the corn and cook for 5 minutes more, then drain the entire pot. Use tongs to transfer the eggs to a bowl of ice water until cool enough to peel. Discard the lemon and parsley. Set aside the potatoes and corn.

## CEVICHE

1 pound cod, cut into ¼-inch cubes

1 (8-ounce) can crushed pineapple, with juices

Juice of 1 lime

1 jalapeño, seeded and diced

2 tablespoons chopped fresh cilantro

Kosher salt and freshly ground black pepper

Put the cod in a medium serving bowl. Add the pineapple and its juices, lime juice, jalapeño, and cilantro. Season with salt and pepper. Set aside to marinate at room temperature for 30 minutes or refrigerate for up to 4 hours before serving.

## FOR THE PLATTER

Canned sardines

Sliced lemons

Toasted bread

Tortilla chips

Seaweed snacks

Tartar sauce

Nestle bowls and plates of the "seacuterie" and these accompaniments on and around a large platter.

# SURPRISE *pizza* croquembouche

**All-purpose flour**

**1 (13.8-ounce) can store-bought pizza dough**

**Tomato sauce, Alfredo sauce, pesto, mozzarella cheese, pepperoni, sliced ham, pineapple, cooked bacon, ranch, for filling**

**½ cup shredded Parmesan cheese**

*Special Equipment*
**Toothpicks**

Yes, there are *at least* five different pizza combos you can pack into these little dough balls. But the surprise isn't biting into each one wondering which pizza is which. (The green pesto will give itself away every time, anyway.) The surprise is how elegant pizza suddenly looks when arranged in a beautiful tower known as a croquembouche. Usually built out of cream puffs with spun sugar draped over the top, we're going full-on savory with homemade pizza bites and a delicate swoop of crisp Parmesan for a final touch of WOW. Part baking challenge, part construction site, part sculpture—100% fun.

**1** Preheat the oven to 400°F and set a rack in the center. Line a rimmed baking sheet with a silicone baking mat or parchment paper.

**2** On a lightly floured surface, roll the dough into a round about ⅛ inch thick and about 30 inches wide. Use a 2½-inch cookie cutter or biscuit cutter or an upside-down glass to cut 28 circles out of the dough. Discard the dough scraps.

**3** Add ¼ teaspoon of sauce to the center of each dough circle. Add about ¼ teaspoon of mozzarella to each, then about ¼ teaspoon of the other fillings. (See suggested combos on opposite page.) Fold the dough over the filling and press the edges together, then pinch the seam to seal and roll into balls.

**4** Arrange the dough balls on the prepared baking sheet, leaving some space between each one. Bake for 18 to 20 minutes, until the dough is golden brown. Transfer to a plate and set aside.

**5** Sprinkle the Parmesan over the same baking sheet in a twisting, swooping line, about 4 inches long and 4 inches wide. Bake for 3 to 5 minutes, until the Parmesan is crisp and golden brown. Set aside to cool.

**6** Stack 7 of the pizza balls one on top of another on a plate, using toothpicks to secure them if needed. Place 5 pizza balls around the base of the column, then stack the remaining pizza balls upward, using toothpicks to secure them to the tower as needed. Rest the Parmesan crisp against the pizza ball tower and serve immediately.

### Pizza Combos

Tomato sauce + cheese + pepperoni

Tomato sauce + cheese + ham + pineapple

Tomato sauce + cheese + bacon + ranch

Alfredo sauce + cheese + pesto

Pesto + cheese + bacon

# acknowledgments

**Author and Original Recipe Developer**
Casey Elsass

**Recipe Tester**
Kyra Werbin

**Everyone at Tasty**
Emily DePaula
Ines Pacheco
Eric Karp
Parker Ortolani
Jessica Jean Jardine
Angela Krasnick
Jailyn Paulino
Pierce Abernathy
Jordan Kenna
Gwenaelle Le Cochennec
And the entire Tasty & BuzzFeed team

**Styling and Photography**
Lauren Volo
Monica Pierini
Maeve Sheridan
Christina Zhang
Krystal Rack
Andie McMahon
Julia Memoli

**Everyone at Potter**
Raquel Pelzel
Lydia O'Brien
Bianca Cruz
Marysarah Quinn
Stephanie Huntwork
Jen Wang
Sonia Persad
Robert Diaz
Ashley Tucker
Derek Gullino
Mark McCauslin
Heather Williamson
Merri Ann Morrell
Nick Patton
Kate Tyler
Windy Dorresteyn
Andrea Portanova
Aaron Wehner
Francis Lam
Jill Flaxman

# index